FOREWORD BY LEO HART

COVERING
ALL *the* BASES

George Whitfield's
Extraordinary Life in Baseball

BETHANY BRADSHER

ISBN-13: 978-0-578-88513-1

Cover and interior design by Stephanie Whitlock Dicken.

Table of Contents

COVERING ALL THE BASES

Foreword

As a young athlete with big dreams growing up in Kinston, N.C., I was blessed with some amazing role models—men like Frank Mock, Paul Jones, and George Thompson. But the one who has impacted my life the most over the past fifty-five years is our own local legend, George Whitfield.

When I was growing up I heard plenty of stories about George, a Grainger High standout who was adopted by Red Devils basketball coach Amos Sexton when he was a young teenager. George went away to college and took his first job in Goldsboro, where he was my coach on one of his earliest American Legion teams. I learned a great deal about baseball from him, but he was also one of my earliest teachers about the value of hard work and the long-term influence a coach can have on a young person.

George is not only a wonderful friend and a great mentor but also a very creative and dedicated coach. I was more inclined toward football than baseball, and George became one of my most enthusiastic boosters through my career first as the quarterback at Duke University and then as a player in the NFL in the early '70s. Throughout my adult life, any time I have returned to North Carolina I have made sure to visit George. At times I even consulted with him about Eastern N.C. athletes as I assisted my alma mater Duke with recruiting efforts, and I always knew that he would give me an honest, informed assessment on any prospect.

George has done many wonderful things for so many people in our hometown of Kinston and beyond. He is driven by the mission of guiding the people in his life and remaining a true and constant friend, and he has proven himself to be an outstanding ambassador for our town and for the state of North Carolina. When a person or a cause needs his influence, George will say without hesitation, "Let's get involved." I'm always struck by his boundless energy, how he seems more like a man in his thirties than a man in his eighties.

It's funny—we're both retired now, but I still consider George a father figure. He never failed to call me after my football games, whether things had gone well for me that day or not. When I played on his Legion team, he seemed absolutely committed to helping me improve every single day. I have tried to follow George's example by bringing that kind of single-minded dedication to everything I have done throughout my life.

As a proud Kinston native, I'm proud to claim George Whitfield as one of our favorite sons. I know that he has been the favorite son for every community where he has lived and coached, and for good reason. But we were the first town to claim him, and I consider myself fortunate indeed to have had the chance to play under him in the early days of his extraordinary career. It's the perfect time for George, who loves to tell the life stories of so many others, to step back and let his own story be told.

Leo Hart
Atlanta, Ga.
February 2021

Introduction

Steve Spivey didn't become a high school tennis coach in pursuit of glory, even though his success would have placed him squarely in the spotlight if he had coached a more high-profile sport. In forty years as the coach of boys and girls tennis at Broughton High and then Enloe High in Raleigh, he had collected twenty-two state titles by 2021 and was still hoping for more. Steve would fit any sports fan's definition of a coaching legend, if only those fans followed high school tennis.

He had won some prestigious tennis awards, to be sure. But few things have topped the moment in 2018 when Steve received a phone call from a retired baseball coach named George Whitfield. The two had never really had a conversation, although they had some mutual friends, but George had a very particular reason to reach out. He was calling to notify Steve that he would be part of the next class of inductees to George's own personal hall of fame.

Steve learned that he would receive this honor at an induction ceremony at Goldsboro High School in January 2018. He had never attended one of George's events before and knew very little of what to expect, but he and his wife drove the fifty miles to Goldsboro High School with spirits high and their appetites set for some Eastern North Carolina barbecue.

Everything about the night surpassed the Spiveys' expectation. The catering from Wilbur's BBQ, served cafeteria-style in the Goldsboro High lunchroom, was tender and perfectly seasoned. An assortment of North Carolina sports legends stopped to talk to each other between the tables, most of them past inductees into George's esteemed group. When the last hush puppy had been consumed, everyone streamed into the auditorium and settled into an old-school wooden seat for the hall of fame recognitions.

Twenty-seven chairs were arranged on the stage, one for each honoree. In alphabetical order, each man or woman was called up to the podium to hear George recite a long list of their accomplishments as an athlete, a coach, or a professional, and then they were handed a plaque that was roughly the size of an end table. Engraved on each plaque, with absolutely no space on the metal plate left blank, were the list of accolades and milestones George had just read.

By 2021, George had selected 582 individuals for his Hall of fame over a period of thirty-five years. The chosen ones ranged from household names in the sports world to coaches from rural N.C. counties who might have thought they were winning games in obscurity. Spivey's Hall of fame class included long-time UNC women's basketball coach Sylvia Hatchell, former Duke and NBA big man Randy Denton and Specialist Jim McCloughan, a retired Army medic who was awarded the Medal of Honor for saving the lives of ten fellow soldiers in Vietnam.

"There were some fabulous people that year," Spivey said. "I was very impressed, the way they conducted it. It was just a neat experience."

Steve remembers asking George how he had come to be selected for the honor, and George told him that he read the paper in Raleigh frequently and he was always looking for outstanding coaches from a variety of sports who deserved recognition. Steve wasn't done receiving awards; the following year he was named the High School Coach of the Year by the Professional Tennis Registry. But he particularly cherishes that giant plaque hanging on the wall of his house, the one signifying that George Whitfield, a legend in anyone's book, believed that he was worthy of being in the company of national championship winners, professional athletes and military heroes.

Similar plaques decorate the walls of living rooms, coaches' offices and businesses all across the Southeast, and each owner feels the same way that Spivey does about being selected for the honor. Friends laugh about the size of the plaques sometimes, (UNC basketball great Lennie Rosenbluth once told George that he wouldn't need to buy a tombstone when he died because his hall of fame plaque would work just fine), but every person who owns one knows that it represents an unrivaled distinction. That pride in the plaques is linked to the accomplishment of the honoree, of course, but it has just as much to do with the leadership, integrity and friendship of the man who put the plaque in their hands.

George Whitfield compiles each individual's accomplishments, orders the plaques and organizes the recognition ceremony, but despite the fact that he has won nine state championships himself and his home in Goldsboro resembles a sports museum, he doesn't have one himself. The annual baseball clinic and hall of fame has never been about him; it has presented him an opportunity to honor the people that he deems deserving and to teach baseball skills to kids who will appreciate the opportunity. It is a labor of love from beginning to end, and its architect avoids the spotlight as he shines it on men like Spivey.

But George's story deserves to be told. Even his closest friends from Kinston and a four-decade succession of the "boys" who played baseball on his exceptional teams are unlikely to know all of the twists and turns that shaped a young sports-crazed boy with a complicated family life into a coach who would orchestrate a lifetime of unforgettable moments on the baseball field and act as a second father for countless young men desperate for someone to say, with his words and actions, that they were capable of greatness.

CHAPTER 1

An Orphan's Road

You don't have to spend much time with George Whitfield before you realize that he is an essential North Carolinian. His coaching accomplishments, his relationships, his favorite lunch (Eastern NC barbecue) all point back to his lifelong investment in the Tar Heel State. Which is why it surprises friends so much when they learn that George was born in New York City.

His paternal roots do extend back to Lenoir County, since his father George Franklin Whitfield Sr. grew up in La Grange, N.C. and started his dental practice in Goldsboro. But George Sr. soon became disillusioned with life as a dentist and sought a much different path in New York City – betting on horse races and investing his winnings in the stock market. He was smart and disciplined with the racing sheets and his investments, and soon Dr. Whitfield had a host of prominent friends in the Big Apple.

Dr. Whitfield was in his '40s when he met and married Marie Rose Tyler, who had often modeled for Saks Fifth Avenue and came from a prominent New York family. The Whitfields had a daughter, Katherine, in 1934, followed by George in 1936. The Whitfields were so well-known in New York City's upper echelons that George's birth was announced by Walter Winchell, the legendary gossip columnist whose articles were syndicated nationwide. George was christened at none other than St. Patrick's Cathedral.

Two significant events, both before George's second birthday, changed the trajectory of his life. First, a nanny named Ada Haines struck up a conversation with a friend one day in Central Park, and she learned that the Whitfield family was looking to hire a nanny. Soon Ada was working for the Whitfields, pushing George in his pram through Central Park while Katherine played nearby. The second event was a tragedy; George's mother died of a heart attack late one night in California, where the whole family, plus Ada, had traveled for some high-stakes horse races. Marie was only thirty-four years old, and her children were three and eighteen months.

Dr. Whitfield was grief-stricken and overwhelmed; he traveled frequently and couldn't imagine returning to New York to raise his two small children alone. So the family boarded a train with Marie's body and went straight to Kinston, where Dr. Whitfield sought the help of his two half-sisters Katherine and Hattie. George's aunts would oversee the care of he and his sister, Ada would stay in Kinston with them to help raise the children, and their father would visit whenever he could. That arrangement worked reasonably well for a decade. George's aunt Katherine lived in Raleigh so she couldn't be too hands-on, and his aunt Hattie lived with the family.

George was about twelve when he started playing sports at the "midget" level in Kinston—baseball, basketball, and football. He loved all three equally and was the most fulfilled when he was on a field or a court. His father only got to see him play once, when he was competing for his Harvey School team against Lewis School at Grainger Stadium. When George saw his father walk into the stadium from his post in right field, he got so excited he wet his pants. Less than a year after that game, on a visit to Kinston, George Sr. died of a heart attack at the age of sixty, and George Jr. was suddenly an orphan. And like so many fictional children in similar situations, being orphaned was only the beginning of his misfortunes.

Dr. Whitfield had prepared a trust to take care of his children in the event of his death. He chose to leave the guardianship to his two half-sisters Katherine and Hattie, but this was far from a smooth transition. George's aunts decided to get rid of the house Dr. Whitfield had purchased for the children and Ada, forcing George and his sister to move into Hattie's large colonial ancestral home. Ada, the woman George called "Mama" throughout his life, was fired and had to find a small apartment and a job to support herself without the children she had raised. Another disappointment came when the Whitfield children were forced to give up their Catholic faith and join the Methodist church.

After such a cascade of losses George was angry, and Hattie was stern and critical. The conflict came to a head during one showdown, when Hattie slapped George in the face and called him "impudent." He remembers reaching out and grabbing the front of her blouse and saying, "If you ever touch me again, I'll kill you." "I had such a bad temper," he said. "It was almost scary to me sometimes." George was nearing his teen years, feeling angry and alone, and Hattie's response was to send him off to boarding school, first to Woodberry Forest in the Virginia mountains. At the same time, Katherine was sent to St. Catherine's in Richmond and later to St. Mary's in Raleigh.

George moved into the dorm at Woodberry Forest, but from the very beginning he didn't want to be there and knew he wasn't going to fit in. He raised enough objections with his aunts that they tried a second boarding school pretty quickly, moving him to Virginia Episcopal School in Lynchburg. Both Woodberry and VES are highly regarded secondary schools, with multiple members of the U.S. Congress, judges and CEOs among their alumni, but the upper crust life never agreed with George. With the money left for him in his father's will and the connections of a potential boarding school education, he could have gone onto prestige and fortune in Washington D.C. or New York City, but deep down he was a boy who loved sports and Eastern N.C., without a pretentious bone in his body.

Lifelong friend Reid Parrott carries a mental snapshot of George in the sixth grade, before his father died and he was sent to Virginia far from the small town that had become home. The two were both students at Harvey School, but Reid was two years younger than George, and the first time he observed the older boy during recess he realized that George was somebody special. He was a boy that other children wanted to follow, Reid said, spending the recess period organizing a football kicking team and wearing the first pair of Chuck Taylor Converse shoes Reid had ever seen. In later years George would talk about his "homeboys," but that day Reid got a glimpse of how easily George formed bonds with his peers in Kinston. All George had ever wanted out of his high school years was to continue the rock-solid sports legacy of his hometown and to be a Red Devil—an athlete at Grainger High School.

George stayed a little longer at VES than he did at Woodberry, playing football for legendary Coach Rock Lee (who George would go on to honor at his hall of fame in 2011). Learning from Coach Lee and getting to play his favorite sports helped make boarding school a little more palatable for George, but he still felt like a fish out of water, and his dissatisfaction was fostered by the family drama that had sent him there in the first place. Still just fourteen years old, he resolved to leave VES, so he hatched a plan all on his own.

He decided he would run away, a scheme that went off with surprisingly few complications. First he packed a few essentials in a small satchel, then waited for "lights out" in the dorm. Every night a senior counselor would come to the door of each student's room for bed check, so he stuffed his bed with pillows so that it would look like he was sleeping there. Always the athlete, he then snuck out and climbed down the fire escape to the ground below. He walked a mile or two to the highway and stuck out his thumb.

Years later, George has reflected on that night and realized that the sight of a young teenager standing on the side of the highway after midnight must have been alarming, but at the time it seemed to him like a completely reasonable thing to do. When taken as a whole, an observer could only conclude that George Whitfield has led a charmed life, even if those years of early adolescence seem to have been paved with misfortune. And the first true sign that things were turning in George's favor was what happened next on that Virginia highway.

He hadn't been out there long when a big eighteen-wheeler pulled over and rolled down his window.

"Son, what are you doing out there? Where are you going?" the trucker asked.

"I'm trying to get to Kinston."

"You're in luck, because I'm going to New Bern. Climb in."

In George's memory, he hardly said three words to the truck driver before he fell fast asleep, only waking up when he felt the rig come to a stop and he looked up and saw the front entrance of Grainger High School in Kinston. It was 7:30 a.m., almost time for school to start for the day. George had never been a student at Grainger and he didn't know anyone who worked there. He had, however, read about Coach Frank Mock, who coached football and baseball, and Coach Amos Sexton, who coached basketball, and their teams in the local paper and aspired to go to school and play ball at Grainger. He rubbed the sleep out of his eyes and walked inside.

The first person George saw was longtime Grainger secretary Katherine Smathers, and he asked her if he could talk to Coach Mock or Coach Sexton. She said, "Son, they usually come in about ten minutes to eight. And they usually come in together. Why don't you sit down here and wait and they'll be in?" George did as she asked, and sure enough the two coaches strolled in a few minutes later. Smathers turned to Frank and said, "Coach Mock, there's a young boy here that needs your help."

Years later, George would learn that Frank and others at Grainger knew about his situation, and anyone who glanced at his rumpled, weary condition could guess that he wasn't just a typical student reporting for ninth grade. Frank told George to come into his office, and both coaches gently asked him some questions about where he had been and how he had found his way to Kinston. They had only been talking for ten minutes when Amos, who had only been in Lenoir County for two years and had two young sons at home, said a phrase that George will never forget: "Frank, I'll solve this problem. I'll just take him home with me."

Just twelve hours earlier, George had been quietly packing his little bag inside his dorm room at VES. Suddenly he was a Grainger High School student, and he had been invited to live with one of the Red Devil coaches who had been a hero of this sports-worshiping boy. Ada was notified that George was back in Kinston. It was a whirlwind of a day, with a few more twists and turns ahead. George got a schedule and stayed through the school day and JV baseball practice, where Amos was his coach. After practice, he got into Amos's passenger seat and they drove to the coach's home on West Road. Knowing that he was about to drop a bombshell, Amos and George walked up to the door and the coach rang his own doorbell. His wife Lee came out, and the following ensued:

"Amos, why are you ringing the doorbell?

"Because I have a guest."

"Well, who is it?"

"It's a boy I'm bringing home to stay with us for a while."

At this point, George recalled, Lee was quiet for two full minutes, before she said, "Amos Sexton, have you lost your mind? Ronnie and Edison are two and four, and you're going to bring another boy, a high school boy, home? And we have to struggle to make ends meet every month? You have a job at the radio station, you have a radio program every morning at 5 'o' clock. You sell shrubbery, you do all these things to make ends meet, and you're going to bring somebody else home?"

The next conversation that afternoon was even more dramatic than the one at Amos's doorstep. At some point during the day, Amos had called Hattie to tell her that George was back and that he wouldn't be her concern anymore. They decided that Hattie would drive George's belongings over to the Sexton's house, and what unfolded between aunt and nephew in that driveway was far from a happy reunion.

Amos and George quietly carried George's things into Amos's house, and then Amos asked, "Hattie, is there anything else I need to get out of your car that belongs to George?" She responded that they had it all, but before she got back into the car she turned to Amos, her voice tight, and said, "I want to tell you something. He's an incorrigible kid. He'll end up in the penitentiary before he's eighteen years old." At that, George saw Amos's face turn red, and he saw veins popping out on the coach's neck. He turned to Hattie and said forcefully, "Hattie, I want you to leave and don't ever come back. And I can promise you, he'll never spend a day in prison."

Hattie's pronouncement that he was "incorrigible" stayed with George for the rest of his life, but that critical word's power was overridden by the force of Amos's promise. George moved in with the Sextons, Lee quickly warmed up to him, and their two (soon-to-be three) young sons became George's brothers. No boy has ever needed a stabilizing force more than young teenage George Whitfield, and with his act of inexplicable generosity Amos let George re-align his life. Seven years later Amos left the coaching profession and the family moved to Louisiana, and many years after that Amos's son Ronnie Sexton found a letter George had written to his father on the occasion of their move.

"As long as I live, I could never do enough for you and the boys to repay you for the wonderful years we spent together," George wrote. "Since coming to you we have lived in three different houses, and each has its set of wonderful memories. I am sure though that the house on 1903 West Road will always be our favorite. We have shared happiness and sorrow since we have been together, but life has so much of these things in it and how wonderful it is when we can share it with those we love."

As Ronnie remembered in his book, "Red Devil Tales: A Son's Journey to Discover His Father's Legacy," George asked Amos more than once what had compelled him to offer a home to a hurting teenager when he was barely making enough money to feed the mouths already under his roof. Every time the question was posed to him, Ronnie recalled, his dad would quickly change the subject, but Ronnie believed that it had to do with the hard conditions of Amos's own upbringing and his unfailingly generous heart.

"My dad had a heart for the underdog and for those who struggled in life," Ronnie wrote. "He had experienced some of that himself as he grew up in a poor Alabama family. He knew what it was like to have nothing. I think it was such a natural reaction that Dad did not even think about it. Someone was in trouble and he was going to help. Maybe George as a thirteen-year-old boy without a father and a mother tended to tug at his heart. I think the reason Dad did not want to talk about it was because he knew he would get emotional. Maybe it was the way George looked that morning, like a little beaten puppy. Maybe it was the way George looked and explained his plight, a scared little rabbit with no home. Whatever the reason, Dad reacted as a father would to a lost and wayward son. He responded with his heart, and I doubt that he could have articulated his feelings anyway. Maybe he just didn't have the words."

Sexton had grown up in poverty, and he had faced doubts about his capabilities when, just after his graduation from East Carolina Teacher's College in 1948, he was selected as the head basketball coach at Grainger. Not only had Sexton never served as a head coach before, he had never even played basketball. But Jean Booth, the superintendent who hired him, overruled the critics, saying that Sexton had impressed him with his personality and determination. That decision reaped benefits and helped to bolster Kinston's reputation as a sports hotbed, as Sexton's Red Devil teams won three state titles and finished as runner-up three times in his nine years as the Grainger head coach. He was not only a father figure for George, but an example for the future coach to follow on how to build and sustain a winner.

Even after the Sexton family relocated to Louisiana, they were as much family to George as if they had been related by blood. As Ronnie recounted in his book, "George still sends us gifts at Christmas. Even after we had our own families, he sent our kids gifts. He has attended not only our weddings, but he has attended our children's weddings. It doesn't matter how far he has to travel. He'll be there." And when Ronnie Sexton died in a boating accident in September 2020, despite the risks of traveling during the COVID pandemic, George didn't think twice about flying to Louisiana to grieve and remember with his adopted family.

As devoted as he stayed to the Sextons, George had no contact at all with his Aunt Hattie after that fateful day in the driveway—until he felt compelled to drop in on her shortly before her death in 1984. George was close to retirement from his celebrated high school baseball coaching career with nine state championships, two national coach of the year honors and a host of other honors and hall of fame selections. He had countless abiding friendships and no regrets, but as he sat at Carolina Dairies enjoying a milkshake he realized that he had carried bitterness for Hattie through his adult life, and he wanted to shed that burden.

"I was sitting there, and felt that I had carried that hate for Hattie too long. In my mind, a voice was saying, 'You've got one block to drive and release that hatred.'" He had not seen Hattie in nearly thirty-five years, but he knew where her apartment was, and he got up, drove over there and apprehensively walked up to the door. "You would have thought she had seen a ghost," he said. Hattie invited him in and the two made some small talk. After a short while, George said, "I should probably get going, and I just wanted to say hello." Hattie walked him to the door and held it open for him to leave. She said, "I want to tell you something. All the people who know you in Kinston are proud of all you've accomplished. And I am too." And that was it. George was free of the hatred and unforgiveness that had followed him for all of those years.

George didn't live under Frank Mock's roof, but the legendary athletic director and football and baseball coach made a significant imprint on him as well. Frank's teams won two state titles in baseball and one in football, but even more than pushing George to excel in three sports that he loved Frank was a mentor of character and leadership. He partnered with Amos to serve as a surrogate father for that orphan boy who touched both of their hearts when he climbed down from that big rig and walked into their high school that morning.

It's impossible to measure the weight of Amos and Frank's love and discipline on George's life, both as a man and as a coach. By caring about him deeply and expecting excellence from him consistently, they set a standard he would strive to meet when he earned his own coaching opportunities as a young man. His former classmates at Virginia Episcopal might have been pulling all-nighters to get into Ivy League schools and achieve national prominence, but George was enrolled in a different type of masterclass. His lessons came on the hardwood in instances like a game between Grainger and Jacksonville, when Amos told his players that he wanted to watch and determine what type of zone defense their opponent was running, so for the first few minutes of the game he didn't want any of the Red Devils to take a shot.

Just after the opening tip, teammate Cecil Gooding passed the ball to George, who found himself open at the top of the key and nonetheless launched a shot, which didn't go in. As Ronnie wrote in his book, Amos "motioned for George to come out of the game, and as George made his way off the court, he said Dad grabbed him by the seat of the pants and practically threw him on the bench. He stuck his finger in George's face and barked, 'You will do what I tell you, or you won't play. I told you not to shoot.'"

George spent the rest of the first half on the bench, and Amos didn't say a word to his guard (and adopted son) until the beginning of the second half, when he turned to George and asked, "Now do you think you can do what I tell you to do?" The coach made his point, George never forgot it, and hundreds of future athletes who would play for George were the unfortunate beneficiaries of this lesson: What the coach says, goes.

COVERING ALL THE BASES

CHAPTER 2

Foundations

As tumultuous as George's re-entry to Lenoir County was, he soon got settled into life at the Sexton home and in the halls of Grainger High. He was comfortable and secure as an adopted son, as a student, and in the role he relished above all: a high school athlete in the legendary sports city of Kinston. As a Red Devil in three sports and a member of the Kinston American Legion team during the summers, George added his own strokes to the surprising sports masterpiece that this small Southern city has become.

That storied athletic history has been most heralded in the sport of basketball, which is best understood by the fact that in one fifty-year period, seven players from Kinston High School alone made an NBA roster, including standouts like Jerry Stackhouse, Vernon Maxwell and Brandon Ingram. University of North Carolina head basketball coach Roy Williams once told a television interviewer, "If I hear there's a player in Kinston, I am going to go there quicker than I would go to New York City." And coaches who focus their recruiting on this town of 20,000 aren't just going on circumstantial evidence. As a 2018 ESPN article about Kinston's basketball pre-eminence points out, the odds of a talented Kinston player fulfilling his hoops dreams are astronomically better than those of athletes from most other cities and towns.

"About 3 out of every 10,000 high school basketball players go on to play in the NBA," ESPN writer Baxter Holmes wrote in "America's Basketball Heaven." "But since the 1972-73 season, 1 out of every 52.7 players to suit up for Kinston High School's varsity squad has reached the league, meaning the odds to do so in Kinston are, since the early 1970s, about 63 times greater than the national average."

George is connected to many of Kinston's basketball legends, honoring as many as possible at his annual hall of fame. And as a former college basketball player himself, he certainly appreciates the way his hometown's hardwood success has helped put Kinston on the map. But he was there in the early days of Kinston's emergence as a sports powerhouse, and he knows that the deep traditions of toughness, work ethic and competitiveness that characterized even his days in midget sports have enabled unlikely success for athletes from virtually any sport.

With tobacco providing the town's lifeblood, the Kinston of the mid-twentieth century was vibrant with opportunity for athletes and businesspeople alike, and George and his teammates were the beneficiaries of an optimistic time in a growing small city that loved its high school sports teams. Ray Barbre, who met George shortly after he returned from boarding school and played on the Grainger High basketball team with him, said that they were blessed to grow up in an idyllic time when drugs and crime were unheard of and no one thought to lock their doors at night. "It was a wonderful, friendly, safe place to live," Barbre said. "Just the perfect place to grow up."

Kinston has intermittently been the home of several different minor league baseball teams, but for the most part preps and American Legion were the biggest games in town, with any professional sports at least a half day's drive away. Just like George had as a young boy trying to find a foothold despite a rocky home life, kids in Kinston idolized the tall athletes from Grainger High School and dreamed of one way donning those jerseys themselves under the guiding hand of a coach like Amos Sexton or Frank Mock. George and his friends never seemed to get enough of playing their favorite sports, going to Grainger practices every weekday afternoon and spending all weekend at the Emma Webb Recreation Center, where they could play pickup baseball or basketball games as long as they wanted. Alley Hart was three years behind George at Grainger High, and he pegged him as a role model. "He was just one of these who was all into athletics, and I think everybody wanted to be like him," Hart said.

The recreation center was an important piece of George's childhood not only because of its fields and courts; the facility's long-time director Bill Fay was one of the first to show kindness to young George after he lost his father in 1948. George was only twelve, but Fay gave him a job doing cleaning and other tasks around the recreation center, then slipped him a $20 bill every week. George understood later that he was too young to really be on the payroll, and that Fay was paying him out of his pocket to help a boy's bad situation look just a little bit brighter.

When Amos Sexton took over the Grainger High basketball team in 1948, young and green but determined to quiet the doubters, he inherited a hungry program with talent but little hardware to show for it. In his first season, Sexton validated the superintendent's hiring decision by bringing the Red Devils all the way to the 2-A state championship game. Grainger lost that game to the Hendersonville Blue Birds in a squeaker, 46-44, but Amos had telegraphed something important to the town of Kinston: He expected to win big. Two years later he claimed his first state title, felling the Hanes High team just months before a disheveled George Whitfield slept through the night on his dramatic journey home from Virginia.

In a run that any high school coach would consider improbable, Sexton won two more state championship trophies in basketball, in 1955 and 1956. He only coached for nine years in total, but one-third of those seasons ended with a win and the greatest celebration a high school athlete can aspire to. George didn't get to revel in a state title as an athlete (he would more than make up for that deficit as a coach) but he was a key contributor and co-captain on Sexton's 1953 and 1954 teams that were Northeastern Conference Champions and competed in the state tournament. In 1954, George's senior year, the Red Devils made it to the final game before being defeated by the Tri-City Black Panthers.

Basketball has long been in the spotlight in Kinston, but baseball and football coach Frank Mock led the football Red Devils to an undefeated regular season in 1948 and answered Sexton's first state championship with one of his own, in baseball in 1949. When George arrived the next year, he was ready to make his mark in all three sports, and he always welcomed each new season when it rolled around, moving seamlessly from the football playoffs to the basketball preseason and the basketball playoffs to baseball workouts on chilly February days. Through those hours on the field under the watchful eye of Frank Mock, George found a towering example of the kind of coach and man he aspired to be, and anyone who considers George's impact on the players and communities where he coached see the many parallels between the two men.

Frank was known for helping out his boys in ways that were often unseen off the field, and as a coach he valued mental toughness, physical conditioning and sportsmanship. In his twenty-three-year coaching career he won two state titles in baseball and one in football, and after his years as coach and athletic director he became the principal of Kinston High and later the assistant superintendent of schools. He died in 1978, and his daughter Frances Mock was struck by George's unwavering faithfulness to both of her parents over so many years. His friendship with Frank's widow Mabel extended long after her husband's death, since she lived until the age of 101.

"When my daddy was sick before he died, George called so many of the ballplayers who had been part of my daddy's life and told them he was at Duke," Frances Mock said. "Many, many of them went to see him. Then after my daddy died, on every single anniversary of his death George either went to see my mother or called her. He was just always there for her for whatever reason, just to visit her and to support her and sit and talk about my dad."

George and many of his fellow Red Devils came to realize, over the years, how privileged they were to learn from Amos Sexton and Frank Mock. As a 1955 article in the *Raleigh News and Observer* about Grainger High's athletic success concluded, "No two people in Kinston are more highly regarded."

The Kinston-Lenoir County Sports Hall of Fame was created in 2004, and the early classes of honorees illustrated how deep and wide the town's sport history really is. Those enshrined in the hall include former NFL players like Lin Dawson, Leo Hart and Ron Wooten, LPGA golfer Donna Horton White and Buck Fichter, the star pitcher on Wake Forest's 1955 national championship baseball team.

Grainger High actually ceased to exist in 1970, when integration finally reached Lenoir County and led to the combination of the historically white Grainger High and the historically black Adkins High into the new Kinston High School. But George and a number of his Grainger classmates have been intentional about preserving the community and the history of the school that meant so much to them, especially through groups like "Red Devils and Friends," a gathering of Grainger High alum that still meets regularly for golf and connection. The Red Devil group was started by Amos Stroud, a basketball standout who left Grainger about the time George arrived, but through the years no one has been more committed to keeping Grainger spirit alive than George.

In a booklet he put together for a 1999 Grainger High reunion, Stroud wrote the following about George: "George Whitfield may be the prime reason Red Devils still exist; the Grainger High School brand that is. George has been instrumental in getting the Red Devils together most, if not all, the times they meet as a group. Without a doubt he owns more Red Devil information, materials and paraphernalia than any other. He is also the most recognized Red Devil in existence today. If anyone has something to report about a Red Devil, you can be assured George will be at least one of the first to be informed. You can count on George to keep up with every Red Devil possible. If there is such a thing, George Whitfield has the reddest Red Devil blood of all."

And his commitment to his former Grainger High classmates goes deeper than golf outings and memory books, according to Frances Mock. "George is like the glue of Grainger High School," she said. "He is always advocating and putting people together. And if there's anybody that has a need, whether it's financial or for some other kind of support, George has always been the support person."

By steadfastly refusing to accept the path that had been chosen for him five years earlier when he was sent to boarding school, George passed four happy and competitive years as a Red Devil, but as graduation approached he was pressed with matter of his next stop. It seemed like a given that he would continue to play sports in college, and his best chance at a scholarship was in basketball. So when six of his high school teammates made the decision to go to The Citadel, George happily followed, with almost no idea of what awaited him behind those stone walls in Charleston.

Happy to be playing college basketball with his high school friend Bert Saville, George didn't consider how demanding a military school would be and how much the rigors of basketball would add to the stress of the legendary "knob" year. On his first night, an upperclassman ordered him to shine twenty-nine pairs of shoes, and then proceeded to step all over the shoes George had polished. And between jumping to obey orders every time a student officer barked them and practicing basketball at a high level, George discovered that he had no spare time for a crucial college activity.

"We practiced basketball late in the afternoon; we ran and ran and ran a lot," he said. "And then we would leave practice, take a shower and run over to the mess hall and eat. And by the time we got through eating, it was dark. And we would go back to our room, and I was so exhausted I just put my head down and the next thing I know I'm asleep. So I didn't do much studying."

When the semester was over, evidence of George's rocky adjustment was right there in black and white: four Fs and one D. Amos Sexton got a copy of the report card in the mail, picked up the phone and gave his adopted oldest son a call for a conversation that would be imprinted on George's memory.

"Son, I wanted to call you up and congratulate you," Amos said.

"What for?" asked a befuddled George.

"I see that you studied pretty hard on one course."

"Mr. Sexton, I made a bad mistake picking the Citadel."

"You know what we've taught you in our house, don't you?"

"Yes, sir."

"Repeat it to me."

"We don't ever start anything we don't finish."

"Lee and I will come down there to get you in June and let you try to go to another school to play basketball, if that's what you want. But you're going back for second semester, and you're going to do better, aren't you?"

"Yes, sir."

George returned, found a little more time to study and pulled out four Cs and a D. He still tucks in his dress shirts in the military style he learned at The Citadel, and he met some good people there, but it wasn't an experience he wanted to repeat. For all of his first year, he had not been permitted to speak to any of the upperclassmen unless they addressed him first. On his last day as a "knob" an upperclassman named Capt. Harry Dawley came into his room with a broomstick and had him "cut the book," or open it to a page and read out the last digit on the page number. Then George had to grab his ankles while Harry hit him that many times with the broom. When the licks were done, George stood up, and Harry stuck out his hand and said, "Hi George, my name is Harry." And with that, George was off to seek a less regimented college experience.

While George was completing his one year of cadet life, Sexton was working his connections in the basketball world to see if he could find a new college looking for a guard. He reached out to his friend Fred Dickerson at Lees-McRae College, a small school in Banner Elk, N.C. that at the time was a junior college. Amos convinced Coach Dickerson that both George and another Grainger High product, center Cecil Gooding, could help fill needs in his program, and soon George was moving to the mountains. He immediately fell in love with the LMC's idyllic setting, and he and Cecil moved into the tiny house their coach had found for them right across the street from the Banner Elk post office. The house was so small that it only had room for one double bed, which George and the six foot four Cecil had to share, but they made do for their first year.

Since George hadn't left The Citadel with many transferrable credits, he completed two years at Lees-McRae, and he almost immediately became a big man on campus. He had an excellent relationship with Dickerson and got to know many of his professors, who invited students to their homes for dinner on a regular basis. The fact that George was elected president of his sophomore class speaks to the way his classmates viewed him, and that position certainly gave him the opportunity to build the leadership muscles he would later need to direct teams and athletic departments. But it was two initiatives within the LMC athletic department that most effectively displayed his extraordinary motivational gifts and creative tenacity.

The first situation involved tennis, a sport George hadn't played since childhood but which he was required to teach to new freshman P.E. students as a condition of his Lees-McRae scholarship. He was doing just that one day when Coach Dickerson, who coached multiple sports and served as the athletic director, came to him with an urgent request. It seemed that Lees-McRae only needed to score a few more points at a conference tournament to win a national cup given for junior college athletic excellence. They only needed to make a respectable showing at the upcoming tennis tournament in Asheville to clinch the honor, but there was only one problem. At that point, LMC didn't actually have a tennis team.

Dickerson coerced George into playing, and the two of them recruited a few other boys with some modicum of tennis experience. Dickerson loaned George his personal racket, and the thrown-together squad made the trip over to the tournament. Much to George's surprise, he defeated his first opponent, a boy from Spartanburg, once he figured out he could play a game of misdirection that would force the other player to stay on the run. "I was in really good shape," he said. "I ran him to death."

Once he had a strategy locked in, Whitfield did the same thing with his next two opponents, making it to the final match before he was roundly beaten by a much more talented player. "He was on scholarship, and he was hitting balls by me I didn't even see," George said. Then he played on a doubles team that won one match, giving LMC enough points to win Dickerson's coveted prize.

Untold hundreds of future George Whitfield baseball players didn't know it, but Coach Dickerson and his prize deserved part of the blame for the grueling running workouts they would soon endure. George had already played for coaches who ran him hard, but that day on the tennis courts he had a vivid glimpse of what a profound difference conditioning can make in an athletic outcome.

George's second coup at Lees-McRae was even more impressive than his tennis triumph, because he was the instigator and because the odds of success seemed even more formidable. During his freshman year, he and some of his basketball teammates started wondering why Lees-McRae didn't field a baseball team. In that day virtually every athlete played every sport, and George and his friends realized they missed baseball. So George approached Coach Dickerson and asked, "Is there any way we can have baseball in the spring?" Coach Dickerson's response would have sounded like a slamming door to most college kids, but to George it was an irresistible challenge. He said, "George, there are several reasons why we can't. Number one, we don't have a field to play on, number two, we don't have a coach, and number three, we don't have uniforms."

George started thinking, and the first solution that came to him was on the matter of uniforms. He was home in Kinston for the holidays when he heard that the minor league baseball team there at the time, the Kinston Eagles, had acquired new uniforms and was looking to sell the old ones. George pulled $150 out of his own bank account and bought them all. They had a K on them and the wrong mascot (Lees-McRae's is the Bobcats) but they were good enough. Next he tackled the issue of a field, and that was a project that required more than money. He gathered up a few of his baseball-loving friends and they went over to Grandfather Mountain Home, a children's home just a few miles from Banner Elk. They had heard that the facility might have some land suitable for a baseball field, and the administrators gave the young men permission to build the field and even offered to loan them some tools. "So we'd go out there every afternoon during the winter and dig it up, and drag it, and drag it, and drag it, and we built a mound and everything, and we had that done," George said.

Two down, one to go. In typical George fashion, he had befriended many of the faculty members, so he went to Dean Hall, who was the head of the mathematics department, and asked if he would be willing to volunteer as the first-ever Lees-McRae baseball coach. He agreed, and George's impossible quest was fulfilled. He created, and played for, Lees-McRae's first two baseball teams. The sport didn't survive over the long haul there, but George and his friends got to enjoy it. George graduated from Lees-McRae with an associate's degree and a lifelong connection to the school, and he stayed in touch with Coach Dickerson until he died in 2017 at the age of 106.

For his final college stop, George knew he wanted to come back close to home to the school he had followed throughout his childhood—East Carolina. He wanted to play ball there, but before he could contact the coaches about finding a spot in their program his plans took a turn. He had stayed close to his "mama," Ada, throughout his high school and early college years, visiting her and staying the weekend with her at her small Kinston apartment regularly. But about the time he finished at

Lees-McRae Ada suffered a stroke and George resolved to live with her in Kinston to take care of her and commute thirty minutes to what was then known as East Carolina College. Young men were being drafted to fight in the Korean War during those days, even college athletes. But George avoided conscription because he was caring for his mama. Like so many other aspects of George's life, the thing that looked like Plan B had actually yielded the optimal result.

George reached out to Bill Fay at Kinston Parks and Recreation, who was happy to hire him back and put him on the official payroll this time. For two years he worked, helped nurse Ada back to health and took a full load of classes en route to his bachelor's degree. He was happy back in Kinston and fulfilled in his job, especially because he was strongly considering a full-time career in recreation management. He knew that Fay already had a position in mind for him – the director of the Fairfield Recreation Department. But then a surprising phone call rerouted that path for good.

CHAPTER 3

Call Him Coach

George was in his early '20s, fresh off of his college graduation and seemingly headed for a full-time job at the hometown recreation department where he had been working for years. But even with no coaching experience, he was about to experience the first instance of a pattern that became a lifelong principle for him: The relationships you cultivate, and the impression you make on others, can open doors that you had never even considered trying to walk through.

His connecting link to Goldsboro, N.C. was Charlie Lee, who had coached him in the ninth grade at Grainger High before leaving for a position at Goldsboro High School. Lee had stayed in touch with George and believed he would make a great coach, and when he learned that Goldsboro Junior High was looking for a coach he put in a good word with the school system superintendent.

George got a phone call and drove the short thirty miles for an interview with Dr. N.H. Shope, and soon his surprise over the opportunity was replaced by surprise at getting an offer to coach basketball, football, and baseball at the junior high school. Dr. Shope told him that he could choose to structure his coaching salary one of two ways: The minimum scale of $750 a year with opportunity for raises if he performed well, or the maximum pay of $1,500 a year with no chance for an increase. Maybe it was his innate competitiveness, but George chose to make less with the prospect of working for more.

Ada's health was improved, but she and George decided that she should move to Goldsboro with him, so the two settled into a small house and he quickly established himself as the kind of coach he would be for the next four decades: Tough and demanding, but unfailingly attentive and caring toward every player who came under his charge. He had played under plenty of coaches who earned his respect in his own athletic career, so instinctively this twenty-two-year-old newly tapped head coach knew that his first task was letting those young players know who was in charge. And according to former players like Ray Bunch, who competed on George's teams at Goldsboro Junior High, Goldsboro Senior High and in American Legion baseball, he was successful in establishing that authority—and even inspiring some fear—from the very first practice.

"Of course I was a kid, but he was really a kid too, when you think about it," Bunch said. "He was just in his twenties, and I was terrified of him. To me he seemed like a grown-up man then. He was very intimidating, extremely tough. He was no-nonsense. There was absolutely no question of who was in charge."

Every former George Whitfield player has a slightly different version of the years spent under their coach, depending on the type of team it was or his personal and family circumstances. But to a man, each one of George's boys remembers days when he forced them to run, run, and run some more. It might have been twenty or thirty years since they last put on a baseball uniform, but those men can still hear Coach Whitfield barking, "Get on the line and run!" And like every other discipline of his winning career, that commitment to running as both conditioning and punishment originated in Goldsboro. "His motto to us always has been, 'If you lose you won't lose because you're not in shape,'" said Robert Taylor, who played on George's Goldsboro Junior High teams.

After three years at Goldsboro Junior High, Whitfield took the baseball coaching position at Goldsboro High School, and in 1962 he also became the head coach for the Wayne Post 11 American Legion team. When Bud Andrews first encountered George Bud was a ninth grade baseball player at the junior high school, where George was assisting that day even though he had moved to the high school. Andrews had heard plenty of stories about Coach Whitfield and how tough he was, but when he got his first look at him that day he didn't seem as intimidating as young Bud had expected. That first impression held until the end of practice, when George took over and led the group in a series of grueling running drills. Despite the fact that some of the players looked like they were about to drop, Andrews was determined to play baseball for George at the high school, so he was one of 140 boys who showed up on the first day of preseason practice in tenth grade.

The prospective players in that big group didn't go near a baseball field that day. Instead they went to the junior high track, where George directed them through a demanding warmup and then told them to run three miles on the track. He held a clipboard and told the boys to make sure he credited them for each lap. The next day only a hundred boys showed up, and Whitfield told them to do the same thing again: The taxing drill on the infield, followed by a long run. This time he made them run four miles. The next day after school, eighty boys showed up, and George told them to run five miles. On the fourth day, forty boys came out. George surveyed the group and said, "Alright, I guess we've got it down to where we can see who can play."

Rooster Narron wasn't even from Goldsboro; he grew up in rural Johnston County and considered himself much tougher than the "city boys" George coached at Goldsboro High. So he walked into his first American Legion practice with considerable swagger. First the players fielded some balls, and after a while George summoned them over to the third base line. Narron put a big wad of chewing tobacco in his mouth, thinking that practice was almost over and the coach was just going to talk to them. But instead, George told them to start running wind sprints from third base to the fence. They ran dozens of wind sprints, and it wasn't long before Narron had to spit out his tobacco because he was sure he was going to throw up. "He ran our butts off," Narron said. "When we finished, Goldsboro High School was off in the background, and this is no lie. That damn building moved."

Even though he coached basketball and football at the junior high and continued to dabble in leading both of those sports throughout his career, it was in Goldsboro where George truly became a baseball specialist. He has always said that he loves all three sports equally, but the opportunity to become the Goldsboro High baseball coach—along with the serious competition offered by American Legion in the high school offseason—made baseball the perfect repository for George's laser-focused pursuit of winning and excellence. Players on his teams soon learned, often in the most exhausting way, that winning alone wasn't enough. More than once, even when the scoreboard showed that they had won handily, the young men were made to run because their effort had been subpar even in victory.

Jim Fields played on George's first teams at Goldsboro Junior High School, but like Bunch he never gave a thought to disregarding the coach just because he was fresh out of college. He had not been in the profession long enough to construct an impressive winning record or a fearsome reputation, but boys like Jim knew innately that it was in their best interests to do what Coach Whitfield said without complaining—even when those orders were exhausting. Fields recalls a night when the ninth grade baseball team went to play Enloe High School in Raleigh, but the visiting field didn't have lights and the game had to be called early due to darkness. Goldsboro and Enloe were tied when the game was ended prematurely, but George was dissatisfied with his team's effort in achieving that tie. The next day, when the boys showed up at practice, they had to run a hundred laps inside the Goldsboro High gym, including up and down the staircase that sits on one end of the court.

Another principle that George established in that first coaching post that became a hallmark of his career was the belief that excellence in uniforms, equipment and game preparation helps produce excellence on the field. Even when it meant paying for something out of his pocket, George was committed to finding the very best items that he could for his teams and to taking them out for supper, sometimes as a pregame meal and sometimes as a reward for a job well done. George's players, teenage boys who often came from rocky family situations and had very little idea of who they were, came to understand that in their baseball coach's eyes, they were winners who were worthy of the best. As a result they started to play like winners, and for many that confidence helped carry them into different types of success in their adult years.

Bud Andrews was on George's Goldsboro High team when the coach learned that the wooden bats sent to college programs were constructed from a higher-quality wood than the bats they had been using at the high school level. In a burst of typical George Whitfield determination and ingenuity, he decided to fix that inequity himself. He created a college, Goldsboro Community College, and contacted Louisville

Slugger to place an order for new bats to be sent to his home. Andrews remembers that the bats were stamped with "Goldsboro Community College," the school that has never actually existed, but George felt that it was a worthwhile ruse to get his boys the best bats he could find.

Dave Odom is known today for his success as a college basketball coach at Wake Forest and South Carolina, but in the early '60s he was one of George's boys at Goldsboro High School. He believes that George brought a spirit of toughness and invincibility to the Earthquake squads he coached, helping instill confidence in his players through intense preparation and a focus on fearless effort on game day. Like the wooden bats plot, Odom recalled the time he helped the athletic director get all of the baseball equipment out for the new season and they discovered there were no baseballs at all. The AD asked George what had happened to the balls and he said that they were all gone, hit over fences or stranded on the top of the school. Odom knew that George had used the high school balls for the American Legion season and wanted his team to have all new ones, so he made sure they mysteriously disappeared.

The endless repetitions of wind sprints and laps, the high-quality bats and balls and the confidence George instilled in his teams started to yield results quickly. His teams at both Goldsboro Junior High and Goldsboro High became known for winning, with George earning a record of 31-8 in three seasons at the junior high and 72-28 in five seasons at the high school, which included the Eastern 4A Conference co-champions in 1963 and 1964. By 1966, he was already so highly respected in the high school baseball community that he was named the head coach for the East in the East-West All-Star Game. The pattern of success that would make George one of the state's most decorated coaches of all time started in Goldsboro, and the foundation he put down there helped make it an adopted hometown for George. But his deep ties to Goldsboro have more to do with the people he encountered during those years than with victories on the baseball diamond.

One of George's most enduring and important friendships was born in Goldsboro from a passing conversation with a Goldsboro Junior High student named Princie King. Princie walked up to George's desk and asked, "Coach Whitfield, would you like for my daddy to work out with your team?" George was a little unsure about this idea and asked Princie who her dad was. She answered, "Clyde King. He's a professional baseball player and he played with the Dodgers back when Jackie Robinson was playing." That fact got George's attention, so he grabbed a pen and a piece of paper to give Princie permission to walk to the office. He asked her to call Clyde right away and ask him if he could be at baseball practice that afternoon at 3:30. Clyde showed up with plenty of baseball knowledge to offer, but for both men it was the beginning of something far more substantial than a coaching connection.

Clyde was a mentor, a father figure, and a lifelong friend to George. A pitcher who retired from the major leagues in 1953, Clyde then spent nearly five decades as a coach, manager or executive in professional baseball, culminating with stints as the manager, general manager and top executive to owner George Steinbrenner of the New York Yankees. Clyde's connections in baseball allowed George to meet many of his heroes in the sport and witness games in some historic ballparks. He and Clyde shared countless baseball experiences, but George's respect for him goes far beyond life on the diamond.

"I often say that I wish, on the last day of my life, that I'm in one-tenth as good a shape with the man upstairs as he was when he left here, because I guarantee he took a shot right straight up there." George said of Clyde, who died in 2010. "I never heard him use a curse word, never, one time, The funniest thing happened one day at spring training. We were sitting there and George Steinbrenner comes in. Clyde gets up, says, 'George, I want you to meet my best friend from Goldsboro, George Whitfield.' Steinbrenner said, 'I thought I was your best friend, Clyde!' Clyde said, 'Yeah, you are!' Then he sat down beside Clyde. He would never sit anywhere at a game unless he sat beside Clyde."

George has also maintained close relationships with hundreds of former players, even men like Fields who only played for him at the junior high level six decades ago, and those lasting connections have only a little bit to do with baseball success. From the time he first became their coach until today, George has cared deeply for each of his "boys" and showed them his love intentionally and thoughtfully. When a coach at his own high school saw a lonely, disheveled boy standing before him and adopted him into his family on the spot, the die was cast for the kind of coach, mentor, and father figure that young runaway would become. And he started looking out for his players, on and off the field, during those early years in Goldsboro.

It wasn't unusual for George to buy baseball shoes for boys who couldn't afford them or to quietly carry out other kindnesses, like the time he bought a suit for the father of one of his players to be buried in, because he knew the man had not owned one. Doyle Whitfield played on George's American Legion team and years later became the Wayne Post 11 coach himself, and in a 2001 tribute to George in the Goldsboro News-Argus he recounted his feeling when his coach gave him a shiny new pair of shoes. "I was an old country boy from Duplin County and had never seen a pair of those," Whitfield said. "I thought they were the prettiest things I had ever seen. He gave me a new pair of shoes and then ran them off my feet!"

The lifelong connections George forged during his Goldsboro years aren't limited only to boys who suited up for his teams. George coached Eddie Stewart and both of his brothers, Hal and Jimmy, and Hal went on to be one of George's assistant coaches in Richmond County. But George also grew close to the boys' parents, showing up at the hospital in Raleigh when Mr. Stewart had a heart attack. For evidence of George's investment in the Stewart family, Eddie said, you need only to consider the fact that George gave the eulogies for his mother, his daddy, and his brother Jimmy. "He was really good to me and my family," he said. "I had a lot of things going on in my teenage years. I was kind of reckless and wild, and he probably kept me out of a lot of trouble."

In a story worthy of its own biography, Ray Bunch rose from a humble background in Goldsboro to a career as a prominent TV and movie composer and songwriter in the music industry, working closely with such musical luminaries as Dolly Parton, Mac Davis and Ray Charles. Bunch, known professionally by his full name Velton Ray Bunch, has won one Emmy and been nominated for three more, and most recently he composed the scores for Heartstrings, a series of Netflix films based on Dolly Parton songs. But when he was at one of his lowest points, it was Bunch's baseball coach George Whitfield who showed up and helped show him a way through.

Ray was angry with his parents, who were devout Christians, because they wouldn't allow him to go to the beach for junior-senior weekend. After a heated battle with his mom and dad, Ray decided that he would run away, and the best place he could think to go was the Goldsboro High gym. He spent the night in the cavernous gym, which was so drafty and ominous to him that he couldn't sleep a wink. In the morning Ray, bone-tired, left the gym and went to school and then baseball practice as if everything was normal. During practice Coach Whitfield walked up to him with a searching look on his face.

"Hey Bunch, how'd you sleep last night?" George asked.

"Oh, fine."

"Really? Really, you got plenty of sleep, huh?"

At one level, George's players were never surprised when he seemed to know everything they had ever done, but Ray was initially surprised that his coach knew about his night on the gym floor. He surmised correctly that his parents had called George, probably because they knew that their son would listen to his coach even if he put up walls with everyone else. "After grilling me, I finally admitted that I'd run away and spent the night," Bunch said. "He said, "When practice is over, get in my car." So I got in the car and he drove me home. My parents were sitting on the front porch waiting, and so we had this little parent-teacher conference with him leading the way."

Acting as negotiator (and no doubt remembering the pit he had in his own stomach when he had run away from boarding school not too many years earlier), George told Ray's parents what a hard worker their son was and how much responsibility he had been showing as a member of the baseball team. He asked them if they would consider letting him go to the beach if everyone present agreed that he would be accountable to behave while he was there. Ray's parents, who had already negotiated through the decision previously with George, told Ray that he could go, and that night Ray slept soundly in his own bed.

"That was one of those times where he interceded for me," said Bunch, who repaid the favor decades later when he arranged a backstage meeting between Dolly Parton and George, one of her biggest fans. "He did that on several occasions when I had problems with a couple of teachers in school. He should be, I don't know, at the U.N., because he's such a good negotiator. He's a great peace ambassador."

Even if Bunch's parents had not reached out to George, he

might have known the details of his flight from home, because he made it a point to know what his players were up to and to curtail any activity that could hinder their productivity on the field or in the classroom. Andrews remembers when the coach held regular bed checks for his baseball players—calling their parents at a set time each evening to make sure they had gone to bed. Andrews lived out in the country without a phone; his family lived behind his grandfather, who did have a phone, so Andrews gave George his number. When George would call the number and ask Bud's grandfather, "Is Bud in bed?" Bud's grandfather then walked out the back door, across the garden and to Bud's front door, where he knocked and asked Bud's mom the same question. When he got the right answer, he made the whole trip back again, picked up the receiver and told the coach that all was well. Bud wasn't sure that George ever knew how much effort the family went through to give the coach peace of mind.

Sometimes the relationship between George and a player was comprised almost entirely of tough love, but because "love" was still part of the equation those strict boundaries turned out to be exactly what that young man needed. Robert Taylor was another one of George's first junior high athletes, and to hear George tell it he was talented and competitive but unable to kick his smoking habit. George remembers kicking him off three or four different junior high teams because he caught Robert smoking and he had a zero-tolerance policy for that behavior. "He caught me red-handed with a beer in one hand and a cigarette in the other," Robert said.

Robert's early teen years were tumultuous because his parents divorced, and the only thing that kept him from drifting away entirely was the discipline provided by sports. Whitfield repeatedly gave him additional chances when he got in trouble, and when Robert felt discouraged and tempted to throw in the towel George was always there to convince him to stand firm. "He came in at a time when my life was extremely troubled," Taylor said. "My mom and dad were going through a divorce, and he kind of just put me under his wing. He knew I needed nurturing, so as much as I rebelled and took the other side of the coin, he always brought me back to his side. He never gave up on me. Every time I tried to quit he would just say, 'You can't do that.'"

Despite a poor upbringing, family struggles and flashes of rebellion, Taylor ended up becoming one of the most successful real estate brokers in the state of California, serving for seven years under the state's Commissioner of Real Estate and becoming the CEO of a NASD INC firm. His professional success was so unlikely in light of his rocky start that once at a Goldsboro High reunion, when he told a former classmate that he was the CEO of a securities firm, the classmate thought he was a security guard. He has thrived due to plenty of hard work and some outstanding mentors, but whenever possible he gives the most credit to his former coach George Whitfield.

"He gave me a life that I would not have had without him," Taylor said. "I thank him every time I wake up in the morning."

In cases like Robert Taylor, it took years to grasp the full weight of George's influence, but other players saw their circumstances change in concrete ways through their coach's intervention while they were still in high school. Rooster Narron, Wayne Sullivan and Jimmy Bryan attended smaller, more rural high schools and played American Legion ball for George. All had enough potential that George thought it would be to their advantage if they moved to a larger high school. (And their presence wouldn't hurt the Earthquakes' prospects either.) One evening after a Legion game, George threw out the idea that all three of them should consider transferring for their senior season. Soon he was talking the idea over with each of their families, and to his surprise all three agreed to come to Goldsboro. George was excited, but he needed a place for them to live within the school's attendance area.

He brought his dilemma to his mama, Ada. He told her he had found three good ballplayers who needed a place to live and he wanted them to move in with her. She had two extra bedrooms, in part because George and Mary Lou had married in 1961 and moved into an apartment nearby. Ada wasn't sure how she would manage with three tall, hungry teenage boys around, but she agreed because George was asking and she was committed to helping his teams succeed. In fact, it wasn't uncommon, throughout George's time in Goldsboro, for Ada to drag the Goldsboro High field to get it ready for games. Throughout that unusual school year, Ada cooked many of the boys' meals and washed their clothes. "She said, 'The only thing I asked them to do was not spit chewing tobacco in my rosebushes,'" George recalled.

By the time they graduated from Goldsboro High, all three young men had college baseball scholarships: Rooster to ECU, Jimmy to Guilford College and Wayne to Belmont Abbey. All were collegiate All-Americans, and all signed minor league contracts after college. But even with all of those rich experiences in the sport, when he sees any of his former Goldsboro High or American Legion teammates the conversation revolves around the grueling practices and life lessons they received under Coach Whitfield.

"We have a bond," Narron said. "It's kind of like you've been through a war together."

Wayne was at the center of one memorable episode that illustrates George's extreme dedication to his players and their teams. In the summer of 1963, the Goldsboro American Legion was playing for the state championship against a talented Charlotte squad, and Wayne was slated as the starting pitcher.

But when the team gathered for the trip to Charlotte Wayne was nowhere to be found. Desperate, George drove out to Grantham, where Mr. Sullivan owned a tobacco farm, and discovered his would-be hurler working up a sweat picking tobacco.

When George asked Wayne why he wasn't suited up and ready to go, Wayne replied that his daddy needed him to work to get the harvest in, so George asked if he could speak to Wayne's father. "I said, 'Mr. Sullivan, do you realize that Wayne is pitching tonight for the state championship in Charlotte?' He looked at me and said 'Son, do you realize I'm a tobacco farmer and the only way I can get my work done is to have my kids help me?' Well, he put me in my place real quick."

George was humbled, but he was also determined to find a creative solution to the problem. He offered to find someone to work the fields for the day so that Wayne could play in the game, and he said that he would pay that hired hand himself. Mr. Sullivan agreed, and decades later on Christmas morning Mary Lou gave him a signed copy of a receipt from Mr. Sullivan, stating that George had paid $22 to a man named Fred Barfield for field work so that one of George's "boys," Wayne Sullivan, would have the opportunity to play for state glory.

CHAPTER 4

Exceeding Expectations

Life was good in Goldsboro for George and Mary Lou. The two were settled into their prospective jobs, George as the high school and American Legion baseball coach and Mary Lou as a third grade teacher at Walnut Street School. They wouldn't have given the first thought to moving if not for the persistence of a voice from the past, an old opponent of George's named Carson Oldham.

Carson and George had competed in midget baseball when Carson played for Sanford and George for Kinston. The two had seen each other very little in the intervening years, but in the early '60s Carson was doing the same thing George was, just two hours southwest in a little railroad town called Hamlet. Carson had been offered the opportunity to move from high school and Legion baseball coach to Hamlet High principal, so he was looking for a talented coach to take his place. He knew about George's success in Goldsboro and he had a feeling that his old baseball foe had what it took to sustain excellence, so he gave him a call.

The first time Carson asked him to consider relocating to Hamlet, George thanked him sincerely for the consideration but told him he had no desire to leave a good situation in Goldsboro. He had only been at the high school for five years and he knew promising things could be just ahead. But Carson decided to take that initial refusal as merely a bump in the road. He started calling George once a week to reiterate his offer, and repeatedly George declined. Until one day when Carson took a different tack. He told George that he had found the perfect house for the Whitfields in Hamlet. It sat right on Kinsman Lake, it was a new construction that the owner needed to sell quickly because it had been transferred to a new bank in Whiteville, and they could have it for a song. If George and Mary Lou could put down $3,000, they would only have to pay $152 a month to live there.

The description of the home, combined with the reasonable mortgage payment and a tinge of intrigue because of Carson's perseverance, nudged George to a decision. He would drive to Hamlet to check it out. He had been to Richmond County twice before, in 1963 and 1964 when Wayne Post 11 had played against Hamlet Post 49 for the American Legion Eastern Championship. That trip had stayed with George for one important reason: Close to 2,000 fans had showed up to watch those Legion games. As he drove around Hamlet and remembered that throng, he quickly determined that this was a town that took its baseball seriously.

George decided he wanted the job, but only if he could assume responsibility of both the Hamlet High and Legion programs. In Goldsboro, he had discovered the value of coaching at both levels, in large part because many of the same boys played for both the Legion and high school squads, and so a coach who led both would have double the time to develop those young men and help them create team chemistry with the Legion teammates who would go on to play alongside them in high school. American Legion baseball, founded in 1925, is both historic and significant for serious baseball players because pro and college scouts pay attention to the standouts on top Legion teams. When he was on that first Hamlet visit, Carson arranged for him to attend a meeting of the Legionnaires, the local group that ran the American Legion baseball program.

There were nine men in the room, all strangers to George at the time, and he watched as they opened the discussion of his possible employment as the new Legion head coach. One of the Legionnaires asked George about his desired salary, which had already been proposed as $100 a week. From the back of the room, someone piped up and said that there was a baseball coach over in Rockingham who would take the job for $85 a week. Then Buford Stinson, a local businessman whose son Larry would soon play for both of George's teams, stood up and pulled out a large pile of cash. George attributes Buford with sealing the deal for the position that would ultimately make Hamlet his home for the next twenty-four years, so it's little surprise that he remembers the words that he spoke to that gathering.

"Mr. Stinson said, 'Gentlemen, I want to tell you something,'" George recalled. "'We have in good conscience brought this boy down here tonight to meet him and to have him take over our high school baseball and our Legion programs, which Coach Oldham promised him. And we're sitting here arguing about $15.'" Then Buford Stinson tossed his stack of bills out onto the table and said, "That'll cover our baseball season, and if we make the playoffs there will be more where that came from. I want him to be our coach, and we need to vote on it."

The vote was 9-0, and soon George and Mary Lou and five-year-old Gef were moving into their house on the lake on Terry Street. They moved to Hamlet in 1967, just in time for George to coach his first Legion team in his new town. The players in Hamlet wouldn't have heard the stories from two hours away, stories of their new coach running guys until they threw up or wished that they would. They only knew that they had a new young coach. But like he had in Goldsboro, George wasted no time in making his presence known as a tough customer who was just as likely to order wind sprints as to practice fielding scenarios.

Armed with even more confidence in his leadership philosophy after eight years as a head coach in Goldsboro, George arrived in town and immediately established the culture of excellence that would produce victories in short order. His Hamlet High teams wore home uniforms in the style of the Yankees and road uniforms modeled after the Dodgers. They even had distinct practice uniforms, which was unheard of for a small high school team in the 1960s. George also invested in more cutting-edge training equipment, including a swing machine that used strong rubber pieces to adjust the resistance and build a player's strength for hitting. As former Hamlet player Richard Knopp recalls it, that machine made he and his teammates feel like they were the best trained high schoolers in the nation.

"He invested into our minds and our wills, and we knew, at least symbolically from the kind of equipment and uniforms we had, what his expectations were," Knopp said. "It certainly provided additional motivation to live up to the expectations of someone we had grown to expect. he gave us the best to signify what he thought of us and what he expected of us."

George's inaugural Legion season, in the summer of 1967, gave a strong hint of what was to come. They made it all the way to the Eastern finals, losing that last game to the team from Asheboro Post 45. After the loss, long-time Asheboro coach Darrell Rich went to shake George's hand and told him, "Ya'll have a mighty good team. You'll win this next year." George took that confidence onto the bus, where Larry Stinson and his teammates were reliving plays that could have gone a different way. Typically Coach Whitfield's rule was that bus trips back to Hamlet after a loss were silent; Stinson remembers a day when George stopped the bus and made the boys get off and run after he heard a post-loss giggle escape from one of the bus seats.

But that day, seeing Stinson's despondent face, George went right to Stinson, a quiet boy who lacked confidence in virtually every area at that point but had realized that his new coach believed in him. George looked him in the eye and said, "Next spring we're going to win the state championship." He didn't mean the next year at the American Legion tournament; he meant Hamlet High School, a program that had never even made it to the state finals in its forty-six-year history. Stinson swallowed hard and made a decision to believe the man who he calls a master motivator. "I didn't have any reason to think what he was saying wasn't true," he said. "It just seemed otherworldly."

Stinson isn't the only player who suited up for both the American Legion and Hamlet High teams who heard George's declaration that day, and he isn't the only one who returned from the Legion Eastern championship series and attacked his offseason training with extra gusto, even while playing other sports. "I played basketball, and after I would get home at night I would take off running across the other side of town," Stinson said. "I would run all the way and back, just keeping myself in shape. I told myself, 'I'm going to hang on every word this man says, do everything he says, and believe in what he says.'"

At the time Stinson was so painfully shy that he put his head down during entire class periods to avoid the possibility that he would have to interact with a teacher. From the seeds of that conversation and the confidence his coach put in him, Stinson eventually spent forty-seven years as a professional educator—thirty-six of those as a school administrator. He was still serving as a principal of Hickory Grove Christian School in Charlotte into his seventies, and even after all of those years he knew who got much of the credit for helping him see his potential. George's big dreams for Larry on the baseball diamond translated to his ability to embrace big prospects for every area of his life. "There's no way I would have done what I did career-wise without him," Stinson said. "Celebrations and trophies are nice, but all of that pales into insignificance when you consider the long-term impact the man has had."

That long-term impact would be considerable for players like Stinson, but before they could get to that they had some trophies to claim. Specifically, they were focused on their coach's expressed goal of winning a state title with Hamlet High. A large percentage of the high school roster had also been on that Legion squad that came tantalizingly close to the state championship, and as soon as they took the field for their first game on a cold February day in 1968 everyone knew that it was a team in possession of a special quality. Talent, yes, but also the kind of unity and singularity of purpose that gives a coach license to push them toward an audacious goal.

And the players weren't the only ones who believed in the vision George was laying out. The Whitfield family loved their house on the lake, but they sweltered through the hot Hamlet summers without air conditioning, a luxury reserved for the wealthier class in the 1960s. But after nearly winning it all during that Legion season, George drove home one day and saw a number of cars in his driveway. He was initially nervous, thinking that someone had died. He walked through the door and saw Mary Lou sitting and talking to a group of Post 49 parents. One of the player's fathers, who owned a local Chevrolet dealership, smiled broadly and said, "We have hired someone to come over here and air condition your house, as our gift to you to thank you for all you've done for our boys."

Armed with the trust of the young men and their parents alike, George led his Red Rams on a scorched-earth tour as the schedule commenced, only losing twice in the regular season, once in a 5-4 squeaker to rival Sanford and once when Coach Whitfield invited the University of North Carolina freshman team (coached by his old friend Walter Rabb) to Hamlet for an exhibition game. "He put us on the field with them to show us that if we could stay on the field with them we could stay on the field with anybody," Stinson said.

George's former players remember that he always had printed scouting reports for their next opponent, even if none of them really grasped how much extra work he put in to compile those reports. And even as he prepared them for each challenge, sharpened their skills and field vision and ran his boys to keep them in tip-top shape, George worked to safeguard them against complacency, against the kind of cockiness that can develop among young athletes who hold twelve of their opponents to one run or less. And in an instance that for many of those players serves as an enduring snapshot of Coach Whitfield's intensity, he drove home the lesson that effort means more than results one night after a blowout win on the road.

As Stinson recalls, the Red Rams had traveled to Bennettsville, S.C. and come away with a resounding 7-1 victory. But Coach Whitfield felt that the outing revealed a lackadaisical attitude, and he wasn't about to let them settle into their bus seats, exultant from a win, without reminding them that he expected an exceptional level of determination for every game, without fail. They were on their way to the bus when George whistled for them to come back to the field. "When the game was over, I said 'Boys, come back and we've got some running to do," George said.

And there on the visiting team's field, for the next two hours they ran wind sprints, foul pole to foul pole. George remembers that they stayed so long that the Bennettsville head coach finally came and handed him his keys so that George could turn off the lights himself. "Coach, I'm not going to stay here all night," he said. "Just put the keys under the bench when you're done." Finally, when they were all on the verge of collapse, they were allowed to board the bus and head home to Hamlet. Whitfield's point was made, and not one of them let himself slack off as they moved toward the playoffs. "The thing he instilled in all of us, regardless of the score, was that you never stopped playing 110 percent," said Steve Winchester, one of the stars of that team. "If you did, you would pay for it out in the outfield."

First they avenged that earlier loss in the District 4 Championship, besting Sanford 2-0. Then they played a nail-biter against Dunn in the Southeastern Conference title game. The Red Rams were trailing 3-1 in the final inning, but Steve Winchester belted a three-run homer for a 4-3 win and a trip to the first round of the state 3A playoffs, where they defeated Steadman 6-4, and then defeated Garner 6-0 in the Eastern 3A Championship for the right to represent the East in the three-game final series, where they would face Wadesboro Bowman High School.

That final series led to another indelible memory for the boys who played on the historic 1968 team. Hamlet won the first game 1-0 and then fell in the second 5-1. George was known to throw a chair occasionally when a loss particularly galled him, and Stinson said that a chair certainly went airborne in the locker room after that loss. Whitfield was furious with his team for letting that game get away, and he would have been even angrier if he had known how much effort it would have taken to get to the first pitch for the third one.

The deciding game was scheduled to be played the day after the second in Wadesboro, but then the area hit an epic spring rainy spell. The rain went on for days, continuing through the seniors' graduation ceremony. They attended their graduation, of course, but they didn't go to any parties afterwards. Instead, they went right back to the hotel rooms Coach Whitfield had rented for the whole team, to keep them out of trouble and focused while they waited for the most important baseball game any of them had ever played.

None of the players is quite sure how many days they had to stay in the Sandman Motel in Rockingham or who footed the bill for all of those hotel rooms and meals, but by the time the rain finally cleared and the Red Rams took the field for game three, their coach had them laser-focused on the task ahead. They prevailed 6-3, clinching Hamlet's one-and-only state title. Because the school would be dissolved four years later when the county schools were combined into one, Coach Whitfield and his team made history in the most lasting kind of way.

They still celebrate that historic accomplishment at regular reunions, always organized and hosted by George himself. He convenes all of his state title teams on key anniversaries, but because 1968 Hamlet High was the first, they will always be special, and they hit every milestone first. In 2018, a group of men pushing seventy years old got to mark the first fiftieth anniversary reunion with George, who was then eighty-two. Twenty-one former players gathered for the event, which featured a dinner and special awards from their coach. Each reunion has given the men a chance to look back and celebrate the chance to be part of something unforgettable, but even more importantly the gatherings allow them to reflect on the ways their baseball years, and the influence of Coach Whitfield, helped set their feet on a path in adulthood that they couldn't have dreamed of back then.

Like Stinson, who found his voice and his confidence by working hard and seeing results on the baseball field, the road of George's career is full of men who translated a tough-minded coach and grueling workouts into a guiding philosophy that helped them become successful professionals, husbands and fathers. As a professor of philosophy and Christian apologetics at Lincoln Christian University in Lincoln, Ill., Dr. Richard Knopp can trace his successful path through Christian academia to the influence of his old coach. For one thing, he said, Coach Whitfield taught him that "you never accept for yourself anything less than your best effort." The other enduring lesson is one that every single player on that team will cite as one of the bold-faced moments in that season. To a man, they would say that it was even more memorable than winning the state 3A trophy, even though one moment made them feel big and the other made them feel very, very small. It was the night that Coach Whitfield took them to task about their lack of gratitude.

George loved to take his boys out for steak dinners, meals that were often paid for either out of his pocket or by the Hamlet High booster club, enriched by the money the players made selling ads for the programs. With their MLB-modeled uniforms, their swing strength machines and more free meals than any of them had ever had before, they were reaping plenty of benefits from their lives as Red Rams baseball players. But as the season wore on, George started to realize that he rarely, if ever, heard one of the young men express thanks, to him or anyone else. So one night after they had eaten their fill of steak and were on their way back to Hamlet High on the bus, George pulled the bus over on the side of the road.

"He began to recount what we had been afforded, that somebody had been providing funds for our meals, our equipment, and our uniforms," Knopp said, his voice breaking more than fifty years later. "He said, 'And boys, not one of you has ever said thank you.' It cut to my heart. It made us feel pretty low, because there was nothing we could do to redeem ourselves in that moment. It taught me the importance of saying thank you for all kinds of things people do for me, even if they aren't aware of what they did. That was a lesson that was a lot bigger than baseball."

He was still only thirty-three years old, but in 1969, after bringing glory to little Hamlet, George Whitfield was named the National High School Coach of the Year. His name, and his success, were now known throughout the state, Buford Stinson was justified in his fight for that extra $15 a week, and the expectations were set for George's next two-plus decades in Richmond County, where he would wear a variety of hats and prove convincingly that his first state title was no outlier.

COVERING ALL THE BASES

CHAPTER 5

Local Legend

Any high school athlete or coach knows that a state title is the Holy Grail, the culmination of a season's worth of hard training and excellence on the field. But many individuals, despite striving toward that end, win no state championships at all during their career. Others clinch one and, despite hopes of repeating, eventually resolve to be grateful for that one trophy that proves their preeminence in their sport.

George Whitfield was in a category all his own in baseball in the state of North Carolina. After claiming that first state title at Hamlet High in 1968, he settled into a pattern in the '70s that made it look, to the frustration of his coaching opponents, like winning it all in the state was a habit. As the new decade dawned and the Whitfields became even more settled in Richmond County, George helped make the county previously known mostly for its railroad activity and textiles into an epic sports town where winning was a habit and dominance was commonplace.

It would be four years before the next state championship win for one of George's teams launched an incomparable decade for him, but it would come in the league that Hamlet residents followed more fervently than any other: American Legion baseball. Perhaps because there isn't much to do in the summer in the small town, fans of all ages and backgrounds plan their hot June and July evenings around the Legion schedule. In fact, the first time George visited Hamlet as the Goldsboro American Legion coach in 1963, he was struck by the fact that hundreds of locals were lined up in their lawn chairs on every side of the field.

"I can remember, as a kid, where the baseball field sits along the highway, people would park their cars on the side of the highway and instead of walking in, they'd sit there on their lawn chairs up against the fence and watch the game from the road," said Brian Moehler, a Hamlet native who played for George's American Legion team in the '80s and went on to a fourteen-year Major League Baseball career. "And part of that was because you know you didn't want to fight the crowds inside. People turned out to watch baseball."

When he became the Hamlet coach, George learned that many baseball fans would stop by Hamlet Memorial Park on their way to work at the railroad, as early as 6 a.m., to place their chairs in a prime viewing spot. Everyone knew that you didn't touch or move a chair that had already been positioned; it was an unspoken Hamlet honor system. But for all of the enthusiasm surrounding Post 49 every summer, the team had never prevailed all the way to the state championship until 1972.

Legion seasons are more packed with games than high school seasons, in part because the players don't have school schedules to worry about. That 1972 Hamlet Legion squad went 35-6 on its way to state glory, prevailing over Gastonia Post 23 4-1 in the best-of-seven final series. But unlike high school baseball, a state championship in American Legion isn't the end of the line. With that victory, George and his team were off to the Southeastern Regionals in West Palm Beach, Fla.

Excited about their post's historic win and wanting to help make the trip South special, the Legionnaires in Hamlet decided to book the team on a train trip to Florida. It seemed like a large percentage of the town's residents turned out to the train station that day to see them off, and David Roper said that even though most of the other teams were flying to Florida the Hamlet group was thrilled with their transportation. "Everybody else got to fly down, but we were all excited because it just gave us more time to be together with us and our families," Roper said. There was only one small issue with the trip, as George recalls. The air conditioning on the train went out by the time they got to Florence, S.C., and soon the players were pouring sweat, with no way to get relief on the long journey. "By the time we got down there some of them had lost several pounds," George said. "Sweat was just pouring out of them."

The Hamlet team, representing North Carolina, notched two victories in West Palm Beach, defeating South Carolina 4-1 and the Florida state championship team 7-2. But they also lost their opening game 2-0 to Puerto Rico and got defeated again by the host team from West Palm Beach 3-2. (The team from the host city can compete in the regional in addition to the winner of that state's tournament.) It was a good showing, but not enough for a berth to the American Legion World Series.

George and his Legion team made their way back up to North Carolina on the train late that summer, and when they returned to Hamlet George didn't have much time to relish his recent accomplishments. A big event was just ahead in the county—the opening of a new high school that would be formed from the merger of four smaller schools, including Hamlet High School. George had already been hired as the head baseball coach of this new mega-high school, which was as large as any in the state. In just grades ten through twelve, Richmond Senior High School enrolled 2,400 students, and George couldn't help but worry about the transition from a small-town high school to the massive, merged campus, with baseball players who had been able to compete on their teams at four separate schools vying for the limited spots at Richmond County.

Despite those concerns, the process of rolling Hamlet High, Rockingham High, Ellerbe High and Rohanen High into Richmond Senior High went smoothly, and the focus and discipline throughout the baseball program's transition was due in no small part to George's firm leadership. And if there were students or parents who questioned any aspect of the newly concentrated RSHS and its athletic offerings, those qualms were soon put to rest when Raider teams started winning.

Starting with the football team that very first season in the fall of 1972, Richmond Raider squads quickly built a reputation as a formidable opponent at both the 3A and 4A levels. The football stats over the school's past fifty years tell part of the story: Seven state titles, ten NFL players among its graduates, and only one losing season since the school was opened. "That first football game, they beat Lee County, and up in the stands you've got all these people from all these different areas," George said. "It brought all the people together. I don't know what it was about Richmond County, but boys wanted to play sports, and their parents were happy to let them play and they were very supportive of me as the coach."

He would eventually lead the new school's athletic program, but even before that promotion George made his mark on the sports at Richmond Senior. He served as the head junior varsity football coach for a while, and that team found itself as the subject of one of George's famously creative disciplinary actions when the players couldn't quite control themselves on the way back from a big win in Lee County. The Raiders' victory had actually assured them the conference title, and a handful of the players would soon be promoted to the varsity for the duration of the postseason. As the players boarded the bus George gave each of them a sack dinner including two cartons of milk. He knew they were in a celebratory mood, but he was dismayed when cartons of milk became projectiles from the back of the bus up to the front, hitting the windshield and narrowly missing the driver.

George asked the driver to pull over and issued a stern warning, but when they got back on the road the flying milk escapade started again. Just outside the Hamlet town limits, George directed the driver to pull off again, and calmly told the players that they were to exit the bus and run back into town, with the bus idling slowly beside them to protect them from traffic. They ran more than two miles on a full stomach, and by the time they arrived back at the high school some of them were throwing up from the unexpected workout. Curtly, George told them to turn in their dirty clothes and get out of his sight.

It's the kind of impulsive decision that could get a coach fired in a heartbeat today, especially if a player chose to record it on his cellphone. But times were different back then, as George found out the next day when he found himself going through the lunch line next to his principal Ralph Robertson. George tried to hide from his principal in the corner of the lunchroom, but Ralph came over and sat beside him. George thought, "Well, this is it." But Ralph turned to him and said, "You know George, I've been studying your contract this morning and there must be some mistake. I wasn't aware that I had hired you to be the cross-country coach." Then Ralph told him that he would have his back if any parent complained (none ever did), and the subject was closed.

Baseball, driven by George's considerable energy and focus, was set to be a juggernaut as well. RSHS competed at 3A that first year because the new school's enrollment was miscalculated, but in fall of 1973 the school moved up to 4A to compete against the largest programs in the state. And the new school's baseball coach, with his commitment to assembling the building blocks for success with each new team, was perfectly positioned to make his own early mark on the consolidated Richmond County program.

Proving he had no need for a learning curve in his newly expanded job, George led the Raiders to a 25-2 record in 1973, earning a state baseball championship for RCHS almost before the paint in the new classrooms had dried. "The four schools that went to the one school, we were all rivals. And then all of a sudden, we were teammates," Dutton said. "With Coach Whitfield's influence we came together quickly. We had been playing American Legion together in the summer. It was different. The first year in the new high school, it was new for everybody. I guess we got away with a little bit that you wouldn't get away with if it was more organized."

The 3A championship series ended with a resounding sweep of South Stokes, with Richmond County prevailing 8-0 in the first game and 9-3 in the second, and that quick series was indicative of the Raiders' dominance throughout the entire season. Players like Gerald Dutton and David Roper, who played on the American Legion championship and then moved from Hamlet High to RSHS for their senior year, said that the rosters of the two teams were virtually identical (with the exception of four players who had graduated before the Legion season) and they were confident in their ability to finish on top during the high school season.

"We should have won it. We had all the best players from four high schools, all at the same place. It would have been disappointing not to," Dutton said.

We always felt when we came in after that Legion win, we sort of almost expected to be competitive," Roper said. "That was our goal from the very get-go, was to win the state championship. Plus he put the fear of God in you for losing. It was always, if you lost a game you would expect to come to practice the next day not to bring your bat and gloves. Because you were going to run."

Those teams lost a scant number of games, but when a rare defeat did occur, the players knew to keep their distance from their coach if possible. Robertson, the Richmond Senior principal from 1982 to 2006 and a close friend of George's, said that you only had to look at his body language in the dugout to know that he took every game seriously and felt every setback deeply.

"He was so intense as a coach," Robertson said. "He would grind his teeth. During one game he got so intense that he jumped up, knocked his head on a crossbar and knocked himself out."

For seniors like Roper and Dutton it had been an absolutely unforgettable year: They spent the summer becoming the top American Legion team in the state, took a train to South Florida to play teams from all over the Southeast and Puerto Rico, became the first students ever to walk into the shiny new high school that dwarfed any of their past schools, and for a grand finale won the North Carolina 3A State Baseball Championship right before their high school graduations. It's no wonder that memories of those two championship runs – and all of the events that accompanied them – are readily accessed for the RSHS Class of '73 nearly fifty years later.

Another key player from that period, Paul Faulk, had an even more dramatic path to George's high school team. Faulk played on the Legion Post 49 team, but he was from Laurinburg and had already competed for three years for Scotland High, Hamlet High's most bitter foe. "You cannot imagine the rivalry," George said. "It was so thick." Faulk knew he had a good chance to play baseball in college, but early in his senior baseball season at Scotland High he sabotaged his own chances when he was caught fighting at school and suspended for ten days. Paul and his father knew that ten days out of the baseball season would turn opportunity road into a dead end. He also knew that he respected Coach Whitfield and had seen his ability to craft winners, so he and his dad came up with a plan. One night George, coming home later after scouting an opponent's game, rounded the corner of their street and saw an unfamiliar Cadillac in his driveway. Mary Lou met him at the front door and whispered, "They've been here waiting for two hours." George walked into his living room and saw both Paul Faulk Sr. and Paul Faulk Jr.

They told George about the fight Paul Jr. had been involved in that day and informed him that they thought his best course of action was to withdraw from his high school and transfer to Hamlet High. George was very hesitant, in part because Paul's parents were divorced and his mother had primary custody. But that wasn't the only issue; George had a parade of concerns marching through his mind as the men talked, but chief among them was the fact that Laurinburg fans and Hamlet fans disliked each other so deeply that if Paul made this move his hometown fan base would not take it well. The two Pauls floated the idea of asking his ex-wife to relinquish custody of her son temporarily so he could move his residence to Richmond County. But he also told George that he thought such an outrageous pitch would be more effective if the coach himself made it.

"What if I get my mother to give up my legal guardianship?" Paul Jr. asked.

"That might work, if she agreed to it," George said.

"Would you do me a big favor? Would you drive down to Laurinburg and talk to her?"

"Not during the day! I don't want to get killed."

And so under cover of darkness that night, George drove the twenty miles from Hamlet to Laurinburg and met Paul

Sr. and Paul Jr. at the hair salon where Paul's mother worked. Paul Sr. made his appeal, and after hearing George promise to support Paul and also hearing her son's side of the story, she agreed to go down to the courthouse the next morning and turn over custody of Paul Jr. to Paul Sr. until June 6, when he graduated from high school. Quickly they found an apartment for him within the Hamlet attendance area, and the next day he was practicing with the Red Rams.

"He came up to see me on a Monday, and on Friday night he hit two home runs for me against Lumberton," George said. "Everybody in Laurinburg thought I had bought him a car to come over there, that I had bribed him. I didn't even buy him a Pepsi-Cola!"

The addition of Paul to an already-deep squad certainly helped the Hamlet team, but more than that George knew that his willingness to give a boy a second chance would yield benefits for his future. Paul showed his appreciation for his parents and his coach belief in him by playing baseball first for Seminole Community College, then signing a pro contract with the San Francisco Giants. From there he coached high school baseball and football at several programs in North Carolina and then embarked on a 30-year career as a Major League Baseball scout, working for the Braves, the Royals, the Devil Rays, the Yankees, the Reds and the Nationals. In 2019, at a ceremony at Camden Yards, he was inducted into the Mid-Atlantic Scouts Association Hall of Fame.

"He just brought more to the table as far as a coach," Faulk said of Whitfield. "He cared about every one of us; he didn't single people out. The biggest thing he brought to the table was a winning attitude. I mean, he hated to lose. And he didn't ever let just emotions totally get to him. But he hated losing, and I was also on the same path. I hated losing. And I hated failure, and those are the things that he instilled into me going into coaching."

Every player on every George Whitfield team represents a story, some with significant bumps in the road like Paul Faulk's, but George always knew that winning a state title would be a mountaintop experience that would follow them into adulthood. He tried to mark the occasion in 1973 by buying special championship rings for each player with his own money, said Mitch Davis, another senior on that team. But the N.C. High School Athletic Association said that a coach was not permitted to buy rings for his players, so he reluctantly had to shelve the idea. But the lack of a ring doesn't mean that George ever lets one of those "boys" forget that they were part of something special back in 1968, or 1972, or any of the six other times George's teams won state championships.

Like he does for the 1968 Hamlet High championship team, George convenes the players from that 1973 Richmond Senior squad for regular reunions. (The 1972 state championship team will gather for its 50th observance in 2022.) At the last such gathering, Davis said he was amazed not only at George's command of the details of that long-ago historic season, but also at his incredibly accurate recall of what each former Raider player has done in the nearly half century since high school graduation.

"He introduced every single player with their wife, kids and what they're doing for their job," Davis said. "Without a piece of paper. That's unbelievable. He always said, 'I might not be your biological father, but you're one of my boys.' He calls me about once a month and checks on me. I owe him everything."

It might seem like Richmond Senior High's bump up from 3A to 4A would create a tougher road for George and his ambitious Raiders program. After all, starting with the 1974 season they would be competing against all of the biggest high schools in the state: Well-funded behemoths from Charlotte and Raleigh. But in fact the 1974 team was even closer to flawless than its predecessor. That year George and RSHS made history again when they won their first 4A state title after a 25-1 regular season. In the final series, they started out with a tight 3-2 victory over Durham High and then trounced the Bulldogs 13-0 to claim their trophy.

After receiving his second National High School Baseball Coach of the Year award after the 1974 title, George approached the 1975 season with his eye on a three-peat. In a nod to the incredible consistency he strived for at every stage of his career, that version of the Raiders won 25 games, the same number of victories they notched in 1973 and 1974. (They lost just once in the regular season.) But in a departure from those championship seasons, this Raider team ran into an obstacle in the form of a rival program three hours down the road.

It had rained for several days before the Eastern 4A Championship game that spring between Richmond Senior and J.H. Rose High in Greenville, and Whitfield and legendary Rose coach Ronald Vincent, then in his third season leading the program and still the head coach there in 2020, talked extensively about whether the field conditions were too sloppy to proceed. They decided to play on, and then the Raiders lost in the deciding game when their third baseman lost his grip on a wet ball and the winning run was allowed to score. George still recalled the dampness, and the disappointment, forty-five years later. It was Vincent's first of six state titles with the Rampants, and it sent George and his returning players home with renewed determination to build a bullet-proof team for 1976.

That year, remembered by many as the nation's bicentennial, was for George and his team the proof that they really were building a dynasty through the '70s. With a slightly longer schedule they won more games than any Raiders team yet, finishing the season 27-2 with their third state championship in four eventful years. It was the first time that a George Whitfield-led squad reached the state tournament final and didn't run the table, as they edged a well-matched Charlotte Garinger team 3-2 in the first game, fell in a 12-11 slugfest in the second and assertively took the series with an 8-1 deciding game victory.

Through that stretch of Richmond Senior High dominance, as George cemented his reputation in the baseball community in North Carolina and beyond and forged lifelong relationships with "his boys," he also served as a mentor to a succession of assistant coaches who learned from him and then struck out to lead their own programs.

Hal Stewart's ties with George stretched back to Goldsboro Junior High, where George coached Hal's two younger brothers. The two stayed in touch, and in the early '70s George helped Hal get a job teaching and coaching at Hamlet High, where he served as an assistant coach. Hal left to take a head coaching job in Havelock, but with the opening of Richmond County High George lured him back, and he assisted on both the Raider football and baseball teams, working alongside George for those first two state championships. Hal left again briefly for Durham High, where Dave Odom was coaching basketball and recruited him to be the football coach, but before long he was back in Richmond Senior again, this time as the RSHS head football coach. "I thought a lot of people would interview for that job and I might not have a good chance, but when you've got George Whitfield on your side..." Stewart said.

Stewart eventually won football state championships at both Richmond Senior and Garner High, where he coached for seventeen years. And he doesn't hesitate to name the person who was most responsible for putting him on the path to his life's work and showing him how to shape young men's character and athletic skills simultaneously.

"I can say this: If it were not for George Whitfield I don't know that I would ever have been a head coach in anything," he said. "The main thing I learned from him is to be there for your players."

Rod Ramsey first encountered George as an opponent, when he played against him as an athlete at Scotland County High School. He and his teammates saw Whitfield's teams as targets in the bullseye – the program to beat in that part of the state. Years later he found out that George was fond of hyping his players up before they faced Ramsey by saying things like, "I saw that Ramsey guy at the beach, and he said he's going to tear ya'll up." After high school Ramsey, with an eye toward a coaching career, went to Pembroke State (now UNC-Pembroke) and secured a student teaching spot at RSHS. He coached alongside George from 1980-'82, and he was struck by the high level of respect between the players, teenage boys who might not otherwise defer to anybody, and their coach. Ramsey, who also helped George with the Hamlet Legion teams, considered his mentor a master motivator, able to pinpoint the right way to get a certain young man to optimize his potential.

"After one ball game in Legion, a player had struggled, and Coach Whitfield looked at him and said, 'Do you have a girlfriend?'" Ramsey said. "The boy said, 'No,' and George looked at him real serious and said, 'Maybe you need to get one.' Nobody laughed. The biggest thing is just the respect that he had from everybody. Everybody respected him. His success speaks for itself, but he didn't mind working hard. He took care of his kids. You didn't realize who was the best player or the worst player on the team because he treated them all fairly. He was a great motivator; he just knew what to say at the right time."

COVERING ALL THE BASES

CHAPTER 6

Side Road

With four state titles already under his belt (three at the high school level and one in American Legion), George was already a local legend in Richmond County. He could have stayed put and coached as long as he wanted to work, collecting accolades and adding new boys to his growing group. But in 1976, he departed from that script in a big way by becoming a master's student and a graduate assistant coach. In Mississippi, of all places. At the age of forty.

It was an idea that originated with Ron Polk, an up-and-coming college coach who had spoken and coached at the annual baseball clinic that George had created at Hamlet High School in 1972. Only thirty-two, Polk had recently made a head coaching move from Georgia Southern to Mississippi State, and he started lobbying George to consider coming down to Starkville to earn his master's degree. Coach Polk had observed plenty of qualities that he respected about George in his visits, so he was hoping that George's expertise could help him as he built his own foundation at MSU.

"He said, 'Why don't you come down here and help me and get your master's degree?'" George said. "At first I thought he was just joking around, but then I thought I might as well do it. I think I was the oldest grad school student in Mississippi State PE history."

Polk took it one step further: "He was by far the oldest grad assistant in the history of college baseball."

Before he could resume life as a college student after nearly twenty years away from a campus, George had to make sure his current employer was amenable to the idea. By now his name was synonymous with Richmond County baseball and he had an excellent relationship with the administrators at both the high school and the administrative levels. In the spring of 1976 he went to Superintendent Charles Harrell and presented the idea of taking one school year off from his teaching and coaching position to get an advanced degree. He told Harrell that it wouldn't cost him or the school system anything, since he would be working as a graduate assistant, and he assured him that after the 1976-'77 year he would be back, but better than ever with enhanced coaching knowledge and experience.

Harrell agreed quickly, and Mary Lou was open to the idea as well even though it meant she would be raising fourteen-year-old Gef and seven-year-old Tyler essentially as a single mom for a while. So George gave the green light to Coach Polk, registered for classes and packed his trunk for the twelve-hour trip to Starkville. George's responsibilities as a graduate assistant included staying in the dorm in a supervisory role, which was in itself an adjustment for a father of two who was accustomed to his comfortable home on Kinsman Lake.

In addition to his cramped accommodations, George had to adapt to a different type of baseball player. Mark Johnson had just been hired as Polk's assistant, and like Polk he was younger than their new graduate assistant. Johnson noticed that George initially seemed to be out of his element with college athletes, especially since the team had a number of junior college transfers who were in their early '20s. "You know, George is up there on the sixth floor of the dorm, and he's in charge of these guys," Johnson said. "And these guys are all good guys; they end up being successful people, but they've got a lot of personality. George is used to the high school guys, who are absolutely scared to death of him, and these guys aren't flinching a bit. So George has to make some adjustments."

As the weeks went by that fall respect flourished between George and the players, and soon Polk was asking George, the king of "get on the line and run" back home, to supervise the Bulldogs' conditioning workouts. He also developed the kind of friendships with the MSU players that led to lifelong connections. "The kids absolutely loved him," Johnson said. "He wasn't just about teaching the curve ball or the double play. He's about getting in a guy's head and getting him ready to compete. That was kind of George's thing; he was going to be there to help them mentally."

One of the Bulldog players – and one of George's suitemates in the dorm — was a young man with a big bat who had transferred to Mississippi State from Chipola Junior College in Florida. Nathaniel Showalter, later known as "Buck," was so prolific at the plate that in 1977 he set an MSU batting average record by hitting .459 over the course of the season. From there he played in the minor leagues for seven years and eventually became a highly respected MLB manager, leading four teams over a twenty-six-year period and winning the American League Manager of the Year award three times.

During the year he and George crossed paths in Starkville, the player known then as "Nat" Showalter and his teammates came up with their own nickname for their middle-aged graduate assistant. Inspired by the intense running drills, they called him "Sarge." George followed Buck's career, through his stints with the Yankees, Diamondbacks, Rangers and Orioles, and many years later, when George was long retired and Buck was the manager in Baltimore, George and a few friends went to Camden Yards for a game.

George had arrived early to watch the team warm up, and as they stood in the stands on the third base side he struck up a conversation with a team official, telling him that three decades earlier he had actually been one of Showalter's college coaches. He didn't want to bother the skipper while he was warming his team up, but his new friend with the Orioles walked down the third base line and motioned to Showalter. Showalter started walking toward the dugout and when he got about twenty yards away he spotted George and hollered, "Sarge, what are you doing here?"

George's graduate assistant year was Polk's second season leading the Bulldogs, and they finished the 1977 campaign 33-15 with a third-place finish in the SEC Tournament. George didn't get to stay around to see what Polk would build in Starkville, but two years later in 1979, with many of the same players MSU would win the conference tournament and the NCAA Regional to advance to the program's second-ever College World Series appearance. They did it again in 1981, 1990 and 1997, and in thirty-one years as a Division I head baseball coach Polk actually led teams to Omaha eight different times. Polk was a no-nonsense and disciplined coach who relied on statistics and analytics before the term "sabermetrics" was even circulating in the baseball world, and in his short time on his staff George gleaned plenty of nuggets that helped him run his programs when he returned to North Carolina.

"Coach Polk was one of the most organized people that I had met in my life," George said. "He was strict and he planned his practices down to the minute. He didn't put up with any foolishness. He had a system like no other I had ever seen, and he graded players on everything they did. At the end of practice he had scores on how each player had performed."

It was never Coach Polk's way to be a "buddy" to his players, but because George was living in the dorm with the guys he had the opportunity to get to know them away from the baseball diamond. He remembers his twenty-three-year-old roommate John Butler, a fellow graduate assistant who had played for Polk at Georgia Southern, whispering to his girlfriend on late-night phone calls while George tried to get to sleep just a few feet away. On at least one occasion, he even set a Bulldog player up on a date when he met and befriended the young, beautiful daughter of a favorite MSU professor.

Since George was sharing every aspect of their college lives, the players got completely comfortable around him, even if they had to listen and mind when baseball practice rolled around. Johnson considered himself George's "protector"; since the situation was so unique he wanted to make sure the young players didn't step over the line. The ultimate test, which the Bulldogs passed, came when Mary Lou and the kids came down to Mississippi for a visit. The players knew that they couldn't act the same away around George's family as they did on a typical evening in the dorm. "They treated his family like they were kings and queens," Johnson said. "I think he was worried at first, but they were so good and so nice."

George also spent plenty of time at the Johnsons' home, treating them as a de facto family when his own was far away. He forged a special connection with Johnson's youngest son Brian; Whitfield stopped by regularly unannounced and stated, "Hey, I'm taking Brian to get some ice cream at Baskin-Robbins!" He and Brian still talk regularly, and the ice cream trips nearly always come up.

Once he got that knob year at The Citadel out of his system, George had been a successful college student the first time around, but the second time he entered a university classroom he aimed even higher. He took ten classes that year to earn his master's degree and made ten As. And in typical George fashion, he also forged lasting friendships with many of the professors he sat under in the physical education department, staying connected with them for many years afterward.

"I think they were kind of amazed, here I was forty years old in a class with people who had just graduated from college," he said. "I guess that kind of threw them a little bit, but they were great. And they expected you to do the work, whatever work was assigned. But I told Ron when I went there, I said, 'Look, I'm not interested in writing a bunch of papers.' He said, 'Well, don't worry about it, they'll take care of you.'

"It was a lot of fun, and I wouldn't take anything for it."

George's success in the classroom is even more impressive when considered against the number of hours he spent in the car that year driving back and forth from Starkville to Hamlet. Twelve different times in the 1976-'77 school year he got into his Chevrolet station wagon and drove the twelve hours home to see Mary Lou and the kids. He had a Thursday night class with Dr. Horn, one of his favorite professors, who knew that George was far away from his family. The class lasted from 6:30 to 9, but on the weeks when George was planning a road trip to North Carolina Dr. Horn let him leave halfway through, at around 7:30.

He would go straight from the classroom building to his car, which he had packed ahead of time with his bag, a cooler full of Pepsis and a few packs of Nabs. First he drove to Birmingham, arriving there at about 10 p.m., and always stopped at the same Waffle House for a late-night supper. Then it was two more hours to Atlanta, where he filled up his tank with gas, then a long push for home. His goal? To get there before Gef and Tyler left for school. "Several times I hid behind the couch in the house and surprised them when I got home," he said. "It took me exactly twelve hours, and I drove it straight through. I never stopped or spent the night or anything like that. I couldn't do it today if my life depended on it."

When the Bulldogs' season was over, Whitfield had his excellent grade report and his master's degree, which would make him eligible for future collegiate coaching opportunities, arm him with new game-day and practice plans courtesy of the coach who could become one of the SEC's best and, most importantly through the years, create some important friendships. "I'm glad that I went," he said. "I would have never met Mark Johnson, I would have never met Ron Polk, Buck Showalter, all those wonderful people. And we've been friends ever since." Both Polk and Johnson were eventually honored in George's hall of fame, and they have been among the most consistent presenters at his historic clinic.

Like many coaches that George has encountered over the decades, Polk and Johnson have marveled at his ability to maintain relationships and bring people together year after year. Both joke about his persuasive tactics, but when it comes down to it the two former Bulldog coaches and countless others find a way to Eastern North Carolina, where George started his baseball clinic in Hamlet and later moved it to Goldsboro, because he is a friend that they simply can't refuse.

"I've probably gone to speak at his clinic thirteen or fourteen times, and every time he would say, "This is the last one. You've got to come to this one," Johnson said. "I was flying out of Texas, and I knew I wasn't going to get any recruits from it, but he kept saying, 'This is the last one, you're in my hall of fame so you have to come.'

"He is one of those guys that can ask people to do something and they'll do it for nothing."

Polk, who retired from coaching but in 2020 returned to Mississippi State as the special assistant to the athletic director, is always amazed at the range of people he sees at the hall of fame ceremony and the clinic the next day. Over thirty years, he has seen the event grow from a more typical baseball event into something that brings military heroes, country music artists and luminaries from every imaginable sport. The core of the clinic—to provide top-notch baseball instruction to boys regardless of their ability to pay—hasn't changed, and George has capitalized on his myriad personal connections to raise the necessary money to keep the clinic and awards going year after year.

"It's amazing how many coaches come to just speak at one session, a lot of heavyweight coaches and also young coaches who want to put it on their resumes," Polk said. "I would think, over the Carolinas, especially, you're not going to find too many college coaches that at one time did not speak at George Whitfield's clinic. I wouldn't have done it for anybody but George."

Johnson retired from coaching in 2011 after a career that spanned more than four decades and included two College World Series appearances as the head coach at Texas A&M, and he rarely comes to North Carolina for the clinic anymore. But he does stay connected with George through another avenue— his role on the American Baseball Coaches Association Hall of Fame selection committee. With such an extensive web of relationships at every level of the baseball world, George is an invaluable resource. Every year the committee considers new potential honorees, and when Johnson and his fellow selectors consider candidates from North Carolina or the surrounding region he always knows who to call first.

"If we get somebody being considered from the Carolinas, I know George is going to know the guy, and I trust his opinions," Johnson said. "Whatever he says, I say, 'That's it. I don't look any further.'"

George has served a similarly valuable role on the North Carolina Sports Hall of Fame Board of Directors, where he has the opportunity to recommend and endorse coaches, athletes and contributors who are worthy of enshrinement in the state's most esteemed athletic club. Often the NCSHOF board considers an individual that George has already honored in his own ceremony, so he already has a comprehensive grasp of that person's accomplishments. "What I remember about George was his broad knowledge of sports throughout the state," said former NCSHOF director Don Fish. "So when we talked about potential inductees, George knew what they were about and their achievements and played a major role in helping to share the achievements of potential inductees."

With every stop on his path, George expanded his considerable network, but only one of those mileposts was outside the Tar Heel State. It might have only been one school year in Starkville, Miss., but like everything else George has done that master's degree adventure yielded not only friendships, but connections that serve the baseball community to this day – all because George stays committed to the people he encounters for a lifetime.

COVERING ALL THE BASES

CHAPTER 7

The Director's Chair

George returned home from Mississippi in the summer of 1977 armed with new leadership and coaching tools and a renewed appreciation of home and family. In the fall he was back on the RSHS campus as the head baseball coach. Each of the next three Raiders teams won the Southeastern 4A conference championship – George never had more than two consecutive losses at Richmond Senior – but those teams didn't advance past the third round in the NCHSAA playoffs.

It was a different story in the American Legion world, where the dominance of George's teams was just getting started. In 1978 his Legion squad was the state runner-up, falling to Asheboro Post 45 after collecting a record of 31-11. The next summer they avenged themselves from that loss in the finals, winning George's second state title with Post 49 when they toppled Rowan County Post 342 in a seven-game series. With that title, George and his boys got to return to the Southeastern Regionals in Greer, S.C. where they finished second overall, coming within one game of the American Legion World Series.

That trip to Greer capped off a decade in coaching that could only be characterized as astonishing: Three high school state titles with only five total losses in those three triumphant seasons, two American Legion state titles and an overall record for the decade of 369-75, for an 83 percent winning percentage. The next ten years would hold more titles, new and significant accolades and a range of new experiences for George, all from the home base of that lakeside house in Hamlet.

In the early part of the '80s George's Post 49 teams claimed two more state championships, in 1982 and 1983. It was a special group of players; many of the young men played on both championship squads, and because they had played so much baseball together they found ways to win because of their unity and their versatility on the field. "Every boy on that team, if I had wanted them to, could have played a different position," George said. With only twelve players, George called the 1983 Legion team "The Dirty Dozen," and the size of their roster meant that outfielders had to pitch and infielders had to catch to keep their winning season going.

The 1982 team won the state trophy by knocking off a N.C. American Legion juggernaut – Cherryville Post 100. After Hamlet lost the first game, the two teams swapped wins back and forth, going all the way to the final game of seven. Hamlet won that series four games to three on grit alone. "They had better athletes than we did," George said. "They had four or five boys starting in college as freshmen. Our guys played over our heads and we beat them."

Hoping to sustain their Cinderella story, the "49ers" traveled to Belton, S.C. for the Southeastern Regional. They defeated North Charleston, S.C., lost to Savannah, Ga., then won consecutive games against DeLand, Fla. and George's adopted town of Starkville, Miss. To advance to the Legion World Series they needed to win two more, but after winning a rematch with Savannah it was the team from Starkville that ended their quest. In an era when American Legion teams played much more baseball than they do today (that team had to play in three different best-of-seven series through the playoffs), the Hamlet squad finished the summer with a record of 34-17.

Scott Altman was a pitcher who played sparingly that season, and as he rode on the team bus back from South Carolina after the regional he reflected on his future – on the fact that it was August, he had graduated from high school two months earlier and he didn't have a plan for college. Then he heard George call him up to the front of the bus; the coach was having one-on-ones with each player in a sort of exit interview. They talked a little bit about the season, but the significant part of the conversation came when George told Scott that he wanted him to drive to Chowan College soon after they returned home. Scott was skeptical; it was August 23, he protested, and surely too late for him to enroll in college for the fall. But George told him to meet with the president of Chowan, who was a personal friend. He said that his friend had a place for Scott at the college and that he would be able to try out for the baseball team.

That was the first stepping stone in a path that led Altman to a successful baseball and academic career at Chowan (then a junior college) and then to two years as a Division I player at UNC Wilmington. He had only played nine total innings the summer after high school graduation and certainly didn't believe he had a future in college baseball, but his visionary coach quite literally opened up his future that day on the bus.

After finishing as runners-up in the regional, the 1983 squad had the majority of the roster returning and a powerful drive to get to the ultimate American Legion destination that had eluded them the year before. It was a similar journey in many ways, with a final record of 36-17, but the 1983 team did what no other George Whitfield team was able to do in twenty-three years of coaching American Legion ball. After defeating

Charlotte Post 262 to win their fourth Legion state title and going 4-1 to claim the Southeastern Regional in nearby Laurinburg, Hamlet Post 49 went about as far from home as they could imagine – to the American Legion World Series in Fargo, N.D.

"He taught us how to climb mountains, not just halfway but all the way to the top," said Altman, who returned to Legion ball after his first season at Chowan and pitched in the World Series. "He was a master at getting you to give everything you had."

In a sense, George foreshadowed that accomplishment, doing something uncharacteristic during the state finals – something he only did during that one season. The team had one game remaining in Charlotte to win the state championship, but George had to drive by himself back to Hamlet for a funeral. On his return trip to Charlotte, he passed a trophy shop and went inside. He learned that they sold T-shirts, and to his surprise the proprietor told George that he could have shirts printed in a matter of hours. Off the cuff, George told him that he wanted shirts for the Dirty Dozen – a design with a big airplane on the front and the words "Going to Fargo, N.D." printed on the plane's body.

When he heard George's story, the trophy shop owner even offered to drive the box of T-shirts to the ballfield in Charlotte. When the first pitch was thrown, George had the box hidden away in the dugout, and when his team beat the Charlotte team 4-1 George handed out the shirts to his wide-eyed boys. "They said, 'How did they get made that quick?'" George said. "I'd never done it before, and I never did it again."

The trip to North Dakota was an unforgettable experience, and one that has created a significant bond between those players and their coach. Roger Maris and Bobby Richardson, major league royalty, served as their hosts, and they even saw MLB commissioner Bowie Kuhn at the tournament. When it was all said and done, George and his small-town team were fifth in the nation, and Hamlet celebrated them when they returned. Sadly, Hamlet doesn't sponsor an American Legion team anymore, but back in George's day those teams helped put the rural area on the map. "The little town of Hamlet got known all over the state and Southeast because of the Legion program," he said.

George was just a few months removed from his second American Legion title when a new decade dawned, and with it a quick succession of honors for the coach whose reputation far exceeded the bounds of the Piedmont area. As a result of cumulative success statewide in American Legion competition, he was elected to the North Carolina American Legion Hall of Fame in 1980, a distinction that is given to just six individuals every year. The same year Gov. James B. Hunt Jr. presented him with the Governor's Baseball Award. And finally, also in 1980, George was the recipient of the state's highest honor – the Order of the Long Leaf Pine. Established by Gov. Terry Sanford in 1963, the Order of the Long Leaf Pine honors "persons who have a proven record of service to the State of North Carolina" and has been bestowed on such luminaries as Maya Angelou, Billy Graham, Andy Griffith and Richard Petty.

Even as he accepted a variety of statewide accolades, George greeted his first and weightiest new challenge of the decade in 1980 when Richmond County Schools officials came to him with an offer to become the Richmond Senior's newest athletic director. The opportunity to lead the historically successful athletic program at one of the largest high schools in the state was interesting, but the promotion would come with the difficult reality that he would have to surrender the head baseball coaching position. Still, the superintendent was persuasive, and for the sake of the school he had come to love George didn't feel he could say "no."

Ralph Robertson was the principal at Richmond Senior during those years, and he has long regretted that Raider fans didn't have the chance to see what George could have done with the team through the '80s. If anyone could have handled wearing both hats, George certainly could have done it, Robertson said, but the decision makers in the school system felt strongly that athletic director should be a standalone position. The schools' first athletic director was Bill Eutsler, who had been one of the winningest high school football coaches in the state, and when he was hired the school board decided to separate the two jobs even though Eutsler had lobbied them to allow him to keep coaching. When George became the second athletic director, they felt they had to uphold that precedent.

"George wanted to be both," Robertson said. "At the time it was the biggest high school in the state, so they felt it needed a full-time AD. I feel like it was a huge mistake with both coaches. There were other high schools in the conferences that had dual ADs {and the practice is still common throughout the state today, even at larger high schools,} and baseball would have been the easiest sport for someone to do both.

"It was a major mistake by the board of education. George would have won several more state championships."

One of the brightest spots throughout his decade in the athletic director's office was the outstanding relationship he maintained with Robertson. George remembers the first conversation they had after he accepted the new job, when Robertson tossed him a ring of keys in the hallway. He told George that as the top administrator in a school with 2,400 students he didn't have time to worry about the athletic department, and he had no intention of looking over George's shoulder.

"You will never hear from me unless you need something," Robertson told George. "There's a key to my office on that ring, and I want you to come up anytime you need to, but I will never bother you. You do what you want to do, but there are two things I'm going to ask of you."

"What are the two things?" George asked.

"The first is, if you ever have to dismiss one of our athletes from a team I want to know before it hits the paper. The second one, if you ever think you're going in the red, I want to know about it before you make a purchase."

Robertson was a supportive and enthusiastic Richmond Raider sports fan, and he was right there cheering for the players by name at every game. But in ten years, he never once dropped in on George in the gym to micromanage any decision or offer advice. Forty years after Robertson tossed those keys his way, George likes reminding him, "You're the best principal that anybody ever had."

With his coaching duties now restricted to Post 49, in the fall of 1980 George turned his attention to a myriad of new responsibilities – hiring and managing all of Richmond Senior's coaches, scheduling, handling the athletic department budget and a range of other tasks. George had always loved every sport equally, so serving as the athletic director gave him closer access to every field and court on which the Raiders competed. He enjoyed the role, he said, and it helped him develop friendships with legendary coaches all over the state, many of whom he eventually honored at his annual hall of fame ceremony.

Alongside new relationships with coaches and fellow athletic directors, George continued to pour into the young men he coached on American Legion fields, leaving an indelible imprint even on players like Ruben Wall who only suited up for one of George's squads. Ruben actually got to know George when he was only seven years old, when he found himself in the second-grade classroom of George's wife Mary Lou. Mary Lou took a special interest in Ruben, especially because she knew he had a difficult relationship with his father. One day she went and picked Ruben up at his house and brought him home to do yardwork with George. They talked about baseball, and from that point on George kept up with Ruben as he grew into a talented ballplayer.

When Ruben entered high school, he was using the same threadbare glove he had been playing with since he was nine years old, and it was too worn out to really give him any advantage. "Basically, I'm in high school catching with my bare hand," he said. George, by that time the athletic director, called Ruben to his office and handed him a brand-new glove. He told Ruben that the glove had been donated by a benefactor who wanted to help a young baseball player who couldn't afford one, and that all Ruben had to do was pay it forward by giving a young athlete a glove one day.

Finally, a decade after he first helped the legendary coach rake his yard, Ruben got the chance to play for George's American Legion team in 1985. Like Altman a few years earlier, he knew that he loved baseball and his coach could see his talent, but Ruben didn't know how to go about finding a place to play collegiately. One of George's favorite things to do was to seek out college opportunities for his boys and take them on campus visits, and he felt that the right fit for Ruben was in his hometown. He drove him down to Lenoir Community College in Kinston, and Ruben studied and played baseball there for two years before transferring first to Shaw University and then to North Carolina Central for postgraduate study. "We were literally homeless for a while, and me and my sister both have master's degrees today," Wall said. "His influence is so much bigger than baseball."

Many years later, George found out that Ruben was applying to be the director of parks and recreation in Goldsboro. George knew plenty of people who worked for the city and put in a good word with the city manager. After he got that job Wall, who now holds the same position with the Town of Wake Forest, sought out a local boy who needed a baseball glove and bought him one – passing forward the legacy of generosity sowed in him as a young athlete.

Whether it was through connections for colleges, recommendations for jobs or helping enable a trip to North Dakota, one of George's chief ways of impacting his boys was by showing them a path to new and enlightening experiences. In the summer of 1983, two of the players on that World Series-bound Legion team got to take a quick break from the Post 49 season to take an unforgettable trip with their coach when George was selected as the head coach of the South team for the National Sports Festival in Colorado Springs.

The precursor to what is now the Olympic Sports Festival, the National Sports Festival was held in non-Olympic years to bring together the best amateur athletes from across the nation. The festival featured four regional teams – North, South, East and West. As the head coach for the South, Whitfield was able to help select players for the squad, and so both Alex Wallace and Daryl Poe from the American Legion Post 49 got to come be part of the event. For Wallace, it was just one example of George's habit of expanding the world of boys from little Hamlet – through trips far from North Carolina or by bringing prominent baseball coaches and players to them for his baseball clinic.

"He opened up the entire country for us," Wallace said. "We're from a small town, we didn't have access to those types of people. But you're very impressionable at those ages. That type of experience, I think it helped our confidence, because nothing was out of reach."

After he helped show them broader horizons, George took delight in watching his former players perform and providing support for them at the next level, whether it was college baseball or the major leagues. When Scott Altman played for

UNC Wilmington, he remembers one crucial game at East Carolina, when the winning team would qualify for the NCAA Regional. The game went into extra innings, and Altman was put in to pitch. In the thirteenth inning, an ECU player hit a walk-off home run off of Altman to win the game. When Altman saw what had happened, he collapsed to his knees near the dugout. Then he heard a familiar voice from the other side of the fence. "It was Coach Whitfield," he said. "I hear his voice saying, 'Get up.' And I look and there he is. I didn't even know he was at the game."

Three of George's boys who went on to play professional baseball competed for George's teams after his return from MSU – Franklin Stubbs in the late '70s and Alvin Morman and Brian Moehler near the end of George's time there. Stubbs spent eleven years in the major leagues, suiting up for Dodgers, Astros, Brewers and Tigers from 1984 to 1995, but before he had the opportunity to make baseball his career he played for George's RSHS and American Legion teams. Franklin considered George to be a father figure; Franklin was in high school when George's mother Ada died, and he felt compelled to go to the church early the morning of the funeral to support his coach. From that point on their relationship deepened, and George accompanied Franklin to nearly all of his recruiting visits and helped him navigate the decision to sign with Virginia Tech rather than declare for the MLB draft out of high school.

"He wanted to give you the best and he expected the best out of you every time no matter what," Stubbs said. One episode in their relationship demonstrates how much George demanded of his athletes, especially the ones, like Franklin, who had sky-high potential. It was a summer Legion game, and George didn't like the effort Franklin was showing. About halfway through the game, he pulled his player around the corner of the dugout for a talk.

"He kind of got in my face and kind of told me, 'If I cut you open, yellow gunk will run out of you instead of blood. Oh yeah, and I want you to give me your uniform.' And I told him, 'You can have this uniform, I'll bring it into you tomorrow, but you will not take it from me today.' So we had our moment right there, and pretty much from that point on he knew the type of player I was and how much I wanted to win, because that's what he wanted. He wanted the best for the player and he tried to figure out how to get the best out of you. He didn't believe in nothing but winning. He didn't believe in second place. He couldn't stand second place."

By the time Alvin Morman finally got to play for George – just one summer on the Post 49 team in the summer of '86 – he had already been watching him coach for most of his life, lined up at the fence at the Richmond Senior High field. He spent hours in his childhood watching the high school and Legion teams led by George succeed, and he well understood the expectations of excellence and dedication that would be placed on him by the time he officially became one of his boys. He had success in high school, at Wingate College and in the major leagues as a pitcher with the Astros, Indians, Giants and Royals. George was the one who helped him sign up for the SAT and urged him toward college when he wasn't planning to go, and he was the one who set the standards for excellence that Morman kept in his sights after he left Richmond County.

"I've had a lot of coaches in my lifetime, but even though I only played for him for one summer, Coach Whitfield has definitely impacted my life the most," Morman said.

Brian Moehler was one of the last players to suit up for George in Richmond County before his retirement, playing American Legion ball for him in the late '80s. But like many of the players from that decade, Moehler had grown up recognizing George as a giant in the community and a coach with the track record to make a young athlete's dream come true. Through his fourteen professional seasons with the Tigers, Reds, Astros and Marlins, Moehler carried reminders of George's leadership – his coach's admonition to always carry yourself professionally, to learn something from every win and every loss, to approach each challenge with the expectation of conquering it.

"He knew that the majority of guys weren't going to play in college and weren't going to play pro ball, but he was developing young men," Moehler said. "As a coach now I tell my kids, 'If a coach isn't talking to you, or he isn't correcting you or helping you, then you should be worried because then he doesn't care.' Coach was not that way. He could be tough on you but he was always teaching. He wanted you to learn; he wanted you to get better."

George had high standards for his guys and didn't hesitate to point out their mistakes, Moehler said, but he never tried to demoralize a player. It's another motivational tactic Moehler has borrowed from him in coaching his kids' teams: Help a young athlete get better by being honest about his shortcomings, but always leave him with a positive word. In one Post 49 game, Moehler got picked off at first base for the third out, which was a cardinal sin in George's book. Moehler ran out to the field to play defense quickly to avoid the inevitable, and when he returned to the dugout after his team retired the side George let him have it for his earlier base-running error. But then a few innings later Moehler hit the ball that won the game for the team, and George praised him in front of the team for persevering.

"After the game, he came in and he said, 'You know, I ripped him apart in the dugout but I did it for a reason. Basically, because he knows better.'" Moehler said. "And then he praised me for keeping my head up and fighting through it, then going out and helping our team the next couple innings. I'll never forget that."

CHAPTER 8

New Worlds

The 1990s were approaching, and George had managed the athletics program at Richmond Senior High School for nearly ten years. He had helped build a strong sports culture at the school with winning teams, well-supported coaches and profitable gate proceeds at home games attended by thousands of local fans. He loved the school and his relationships with colleagues and students, which is why he surprised himself as much as anybody one day in 1989 when he decided it was time to retire.

That afternoon during a free period he had played tennis with Raiders football coach Daryl Barnes, something he had done dozens of times before. Barnes hit a ball past him and George walked over to retrieve it. "I went back to get that ball," George said. "And I grabbed that ball and I looked at it, and I said, 'You know, Coach, it's about time to hang it up.' And I knew right then for some reason. It's almost like the good Lord told me it was time to go. And a few days later I went in and told them that 1990 would be my last year.

"Before I went to school that day, it had never crossed my mind. Never. It was crazy."

He didn't know what was ahead for him, but George knew suddenly with crystal clarity that he had done what he came to Richmond County to do. The athletic programs were in good shape, there was plenty of money in the bank and as a coach he had reached the top of the mountain many times: One state championship with Hamlet High, three with Richmond Senior and four state titles and one World Series trip with Hamlet Post 49. It was the perfect time to make his exit.

With twenty-three years spent in Richmond County as a baseball coach and athletic director, George and his family would have surprised no one if they had stayed in the community after retirement. In fact, during his earlier years there George assumed that they would do exactly that. But as his final days at the high school drew nearer, the Whitfields decided that it would be best if they moved back to Goldsboro. So as the 1989-'90 spring sports seasons and the school year concluded, a generation of kids who had never known anything than Coach Whitfield at the center of their baseball world had to say goodbye.

That spring, George's friends at the high school and beyond—men who had played for him over three decades, their families, friends, fans and others – packed into the Richmond High cafeteria for a tribute and going-away party. They presented George with a huge plaque, made from a refinished piece of cherry wood taken from an old barn in Hamlet and emblazoned with a full rundown of everything he had done since he pulled into Hamlet in 1967 as a young newcomer coach who almost didn't get hired because some Legionnaires thought his salary requirements were too high.

"This county lost a diamond when we lost him," said Scott Altman, who played on George's state champion Legion teams in the early '80s. "He had such an impact on this community, he did so much for people. He could never be repaid for all these boys who are now men."

George packed up nearly a quarter-century of memories and belongings and headed back to Goldsboro, the place where his coaching career had commenced so long ago. He was only fifty-three years old and he had every intention of working again somewhere else, but he had a sense that he should wait to see which opportunities presented themselves. As it turned out, four different doors would open in his next decade – each more interesting and challenging than the last.

His first new job, which came about shortly after he returned to Goldsboro, was the most out of character for the man who seemed born to coach and supervise coaches. His former player Rooster Narron, who had suited up for him on the Goldsboro American Legion squad and then transferred to Goldsboro High as a senior with two of his teammates and lived with George's mother, had a sports equipment company called Sportsman's World, and he hired his old mentor as a sales representative. George traveled around the state, calling on coaches and pitching Sportsman's World products. There were elements of the job he enjoyed: The travel, the conversations, reconnections with old friends he had coached against. But the gig lasted less than a year. George was gifted at motivating people to perform at their highest level, but he didn't feel passionate about motivating them to buy something.

In 1991, soon after he left Sportsman's World, George learned that Mount Olive College, the small Baptist college fifteen miles from Goldsboro, was looking for a new athletic director. George felt that a position there could provide a good outlet for his past experience and an excellent use for his master's degree. He presented the idea to Clyde King, who gave his support, and then sent his résumé to long-time Mount Olive president Dr. Burkette Raper. It wasn't long before Raper had called and offered George the AD position, and for the second time he made the shift from high school hallways to collegiate walkways.

George's new job meant that he would be Carl Lancaster's boss, since Carl had been named the Trojans head baseball coach in 1987. The two had crossed paths before and had a history of affection and respect. As a young player in Wayne County, Carl had watched George's teams amass wins and wished he could have the chance to play for him, and a few years later, as the young head coach at Eastern Wayne, Carl had coached against George when his team faced Richmond Senior. Carl looked up to George as a coach and mentor and was thrilled at the prospect of working with him – once he was able to dismiss an early misunderstanding.

When he heard who his new athletic director was going to be, he was struck by the realization that he would be supervised by one of the best baseball coaches the state had seen, and he couldn't help but wonder if George would want to get back into coaching. "I asked George if we could have a meeting, and I said, 'What are your intentions?'" Lancaster said. "I thought he was coming to take my job." George quickly reassured him that he was coming to Mount Olive to be the athletic director and to support Carl in any way he could – to provide a framework so Carl could focus on coaching a winner. A year later the two were in Des Moines, Iowa, where Carl was coaching Mount Olive in the NAIA World Series.

That 1992 postseason, which featured the Trojans winning the NAIA Regional in Lexington, Ky. and then heading to Des Moines, Iowa for the World Series, was a memorable experience for both men, and Carl marveled at George's careful planning and his determination to take care of logistics so Carl's attention wouldn't be diverted from coaching.

"He said, 'I'll take care of everything; all you've got to do is coach your team,'" Lancaster said. "He gave me an itinerary of when the bus would arrive, what time we would get on it, where we would stop for lunch. He had it all planned out, even to stopping at the University of Kentucky on the way to our final regional game for a practice at their facility. It was just crazy. I'm at Kentucky practicing on that field, and I'm thinking, 'This is unbelievable.'"

In a callback to that day in Charlotte when George bought custom T-shirts for his Hamlet Legion 4 team before they had even clinched the state championship, he reserved the back room of a Lexington restaurant for the Mount Olive team and even had special gifts for Lancaster, his assistant coach and their wives to commemorate their regional title. But the gifts and the restaurant were all lined up before the Trojans had won the final game. "I don't know how he had time to make this happen," Lancaster said.

Besides the opportunity to create once-in-a-lifetime experiences for his teams who advanced in the postseason, one of George's favorite parts of the Mount Olive job was the class he was able to teach about coaching principles and ethics. Instead of traditional textbooks, he charged his students to read a number of biographies of successful coaches – men like Jim Valvano, Dave Odom, Dean Smith, Bear Bryant, John Wooden and Casey Stengel – and report to the class about the high and low points of that coach's career and what had made his team stand out.

George stayed at Mount Olive from 1991 to 1993, but he wasn't convinced it was the place where he was meant to retire. When he left that post he didn't have another job lined up, but while he considered his next steps he could have made a part-time job out of attending hall of fame inductions. Three different distinguished bodies tapped him for membership that year: the American Baseball Coaches Association Hall of Fame in early January, the Goldsboro High School Hall of Fame in late January, and the North Carolina High School Athletic Directors Hall of Fame in April.

Never one to sit still, George rolled right from that succession of accolades into another enticing job opportunity. In 1994 Dr. Charles Russell from Pitt Community College in Greenville asked him to consider taking the school's open athletic director position. When George took over at PCC, he was only managing two sports – softball and basketball. Naturally, he had one chief goal for his new junior college home – a baseball program. He brought it up with Dr. Russell at his interview and virtually every time they talked after that and he always got the same answer: PCC could not start baseball because they didn't have the money for a field, uniforms, coaches' salaries, travel and every other cost a baseball program would incur.

It seems that nobody told Dr. Charles Russell about the time a young George Whitfield conjured a baseball program seemingly out of thin air at Lees-McRae College. And this time he wasn't a college kid with few connections; he was an eight-time state champion who had just been inducted into the three halls of fame, and he was the athletic director for a college that was important to some of Pitt County's most prominent business leaders. He went out knocking on doors, and in one happy day he was handed two $50,000 checks – one from Jimmy and Connie Bond representing the Minges family that owned the local Pepsi bottling company, and one from Parker Overton, who had started a successful retail sporting goods operation.

Armed with two small pieces of paper representing a $100,000 investment in Pitt Community College baseball, George knocked on Dr. Russell's door one afternoon. "He said, 'Come in, coach!" George said. "And I leaned over the desk and threw $100,000 up on his desk. He looked at them and said, 'Go get 'em, boy.'"

George made himself the head coach and hired former ECU coach Monte Little as his assistant. George had coached Monte nearly thirty years earlier as the head coach of the East Team for the East/West All-Star Game when Little, a talented player from Ayden, had been selected for the victorious East squad. The two set about on their most daunting task: Recruiting a deep, talented team for a program with no history, no legacy, no dorms and no home stadium. (Ground had been broken on the Minges-Overton Baseball Complex on campus, but for the Bulldogs' first 1996 season they would have to play at Guy Smith Stadium, a facility in Greenville used primarily for youth baseball.) They reached out to scouts who were already well-versed in the high school talent in the area and used the extensive web of contacts both of them had developed in the baseball world to find the right kind of players for their unusual venture.

Their recruiting pitch went something like this: If you play baseball for the Bulldogs, you'll have the opportunity to build something great from the ground up. You can develop your game for two years, and after that time you'll be more than equipped to either transfer to a Division I program or sign with a major league organization. Soon they had a full roster of strong players, many of whom were getting offers from four-year colleges. Even as the college baseball world at large wasn't even aware that PCC had a baseball team, that upstart program was stealing players out from under the noses of programs like Virginia and N.C. State. George was tremendously persuasive, as Cory Scott recalls. A gifted young pitcher from Currituck County, Cory had been drafted in the 40th round of the MLB draft by the Baltimore Orioles but thought he might want to test the college waters. He had received interest from at least a half a dozen Division I schools in the Southeast but still felt adrift about how to make his decision. Until George Whitfield knocked on his door.

"He comes to my house, meets my parents, he sits down with my parents and discusses me, my life, my career, where I could go, what I mean to him, what all his kids mean to him,"

Cory said. "I hugged him when he left, then told my mom and dad, that's where I want to go. You know they always say first impressions mean a lot? Coach Whitfield put one on me that I'll never forget. Coach Whitfield told me that I had the opportunity to go there and be his number one guy. And he's never told me anything that's not true."

As George and Monte started logging commitments from players like Cory, they continued fundraising efforts—selling fence signs to local companies to help subsidize the cost of the new field and soliciting other donations to cover the costs of travel and lodging for away games. George also realized that he needed to make a solid plan for the athletes' lodging once they arrived on campus. Since PCC is a community college with no student housing, George visited an apartment complex near the college and talked with the manager about reserving a block of sixteen apartments for the baseball players to rent. It seemed like an excellent idea at the time, he said; everyone living together, sharing life, developing team unity. But shortly after the guys moved in, George was awakened one night by a 3 a.m. phone call from the apartment manager.

"George, you're going to have to come out here," she told the coach. "The boys are out here in the carport area cooking steaks in the middle of the night, and there are beer cans and Pepsi cans everywhere. If this is the kind of activity some of them are going to do we aren't going to be able to have them here anymore."

As quickly as he could, George put on clothes and shoes and drove over to the apartments. When he arrived, he was stunned to find that the area where the party had been was deserted and completely cleaned up. Aware that they were about to be caught red-handed, the players had discarded the evidence. But that quick action only prolonged the confrontation to the next day – when George looked them all squarely in the eye at practice.

"I told them, 'I'm trying to put you in a nice place, but you're going to get moved out if you party all night," he said. "Then I asked them, 'Who's the ringleader of this outfit?'"

Slowly and sheepishly, Cory raised his hand. George told him that for the next two weeks, Cory would have to report to the field every morning at 5 a.m. to run, as punishment for the incident. George would be punished too, he told him, since he would have to get up at the crack of dawn to supervise him, but it would remind him of the standards of the program whose uniform he would soon wear. Cory did his penance, thrived at PCC and eventually transferred to East Carolina, where he was an All-American.

Even though that late-night phone call and the subsequent two weeks of early mornings made George wonder if he had made a huge mistake in arranging his team's housing, Scott said that the living arrangement turned out to be a secret ingredient of the Bulldogs' successful inaugural season, and a key reason why the guys on that team, now men in their forties with families, have stayed incredibly close. "He stuck all the 18- and 19-year-old boys in one building, right out of high school, with no parents," Scott said. "But you know what? That was the special part of it. All of us were right there together, we stayed together, we did everything together. And it showed out on the field. We were a team, we were brothers, and we played like it."

As his punishment for Scott's "leadership" in the late-night cookout indicates, George didn't mellow in the later years of his coaching career about the importance of pushing players to their limit and instilling discipline in a quest to produce excellence. He celebrated his sixtieth birthday while he was at PCC, but he was still every bit the "get on the line and run" coach. And in one unexpected workout that those men will never forget, he was the "run back from McDonald's" coach.

George told the players that they were going to take the

PCC van to Kinston to see the minor-league Kinston Indians play, but his specific directive for them to wear tennis shoes should have given them pause. He drove the team down N.C. 11 South toward Kinston, but while they were still in Pitt County he pulled over at the McDonald's in Ayden and told them to hop out of the van. Then he said, "See ya'll when you get back." Instead of watching a baseball game, the players were going to run the nine miles back up N.C. 11 to the college, while he monitored them from the van all the way. "He drove up and down the highway, watching us, to make sure we were running," Scott said.

"He was a very demanding coach, he was very disciplined, and he expected the best out of his players," said Little.

So many of the players on that team had been the shining stars of their high school squads; nine of them had been drafted out of high school and opted to go play for George instead. They were young and a bit cocky and didn't really think they needed nine-mile runs along the highway, Cory said, but Coach Whitfield taught them otherwise. And from both an individual and team standpoint, his approach once again paid off. The intentional recruiting, the grueling conditioning, the community apartment complex and George's steady leadership combined for a historic result. That 1996 PCC team finished the season 34-16, which was the best record ever for a junior college team in its first year of existence.

Even though he never actually played a game for PCC, Jamie Stallings credits George's leadership that season—and that exceptionally close-knit squad—with setting him on an unexpected career course in baseball. Jamie had met George at his clinic, and at George's urging he came to PCC as a preferred walk-on in the fall of 1995. But Jamie tore his labrum in the preseason, effectively ending his playing career. He considered going home to La Grange, but George urged him to stay on as his special assistant, and in that role he learned the fundamentals from the best and made lifelong friends from that Bulldogs squad. Nine years later George brought Jamie on board as an assistant when he coached at Arendell Parrott Academy, and four years after that Jamie was hired as an associate scout for the Philadelphia Phillies.

"I don't think I've ever met anyone as motivating as him," Stallings said of George and his key role as a baseball mentor. "I always wanted to be someone that the youth could look up to confide in just like he was. He always had a magical way of telling you what you needed to hear when you needed to hear it.

"Everything I've been able to accomplish in the game of baseball, it all goes back to him."

As the '96-'97 season approached, George received a diagnosis of prostate cancer and needed to undergo surgery. Although he and Little worked together in the summer and preseason to prepare for the second-ever PCC season, George decided to step down and leave the program in Monte's hands for the 1997 schedule. He had enjoyed the chance to be a pioneer and start something that has continued with an eye toward excellence under current coach Tommy Eason, who led the Bulldogs to the NJCAA World Series in 2010 and 2017. George slowed down for a while as he recovered physically, but absolutely no one was surprised when he was soon presented with an opportunity he accepted on the spot.

COVERING ALL THE BASES

CHAPTER 9

Pirate Country

In the fall of 1997 George was sixty-one years old and more than entitled to start slowing down. He had been toiling away on baseball fields and athletic director's offices for close to forty years, and he had recently undergone a successful battle with prostate cancer. From his home in Greenville, he was trying to take it easy as the doctor had prescribed, but his innate resistance to inactivity made it difficult. George was born to interact, to encourage, to lead, to do, and with the cancer beaten back he couldn't imagine sitting around and watching television much longer.

The truth is, he wanted something meaningful to do, a challenge different from the ones he had already undertaken. If someone had pressed him on the one job he had not yet held but desperately wanted to tackle, he likely would have said that he aspired to coach Division I college baseball. But that dream seemed far-fetched – until a surprise phone call one morning brought it right to his doorstep.

The coach on the other end of the phone line was Keith LeClair, who had recently been named the new head baseball coach at East Carolina University. Only thirty-one, LeClair had already made a splash in Division I baseball as the head coach at Western Carolina. After being the youngest Division I head coach in the nation when he took over at WCU at the age of twenty-five, LeClair brought the Catamounts within one run of the College World Series in 1993. The ECU administration had hired him in hopes of boosting a baseball program that had finished no higher than fourth in the Colonial Athletic Conference standings in the past three seasons.

George had met Keith a few years earlier at George's baseball clinic in Richmond County, and the seasoned coach had made an impression. They might have been thirty years apart, but they shared a love for tough, blue-collar players and a conditioning regimen designed to make sure nobody could outlast their team. LeClair had brought in two young assistants he knew well – Todd Raleigh and Randy Mazey – and the NCAA didn't allow any more funds for assistants. But he felt like his staff needed another dimension, and when he realized that George was sitting just a few blocks away, supposedly retired, he knew what he wanted to do. That surprise phone call is seared in George's brain:

"George, I was wondering if you might be able to drop by my office," Keith said. "I would love to say hello to you. What are you doing right now?"

"Well right now I'm eating a bowl of cornflakes," George said.

"When you're finished do you think you could come over here?"

In just a few minutes George had finished his breakfast, hopped in his car and made his way to the ECU baseball offices. He still wasn't clear about the purpose of the visit, but Keith didn't waste any time getting to the point.

"He got up from his desk and went up and closed the door, and I thought, 'What's going on?'" George said. "And he said,

'Coach, the reason that I called you over here is that I would really like for you to consider helping me out. We cannot pay but two coaches besides the head coach, so there's not going to be any salary in it, but all your expenses, I can work with you on that. But I would love to have you do it.'

"And I looked straight at him and I said, 'Keith, you know, I don't usually make quick decisions about anything, but I think I would love to do that.'"

Soon the two had reached an agreement for George to become an official, if volunteer, assistant coach for the Pirates. Even if he didn't draw a paycheck, he was every bit a member of the staff, and the players from that era felt that each ECU coach pushed them and inspired them in his own distinct way. "Coach Whit showed up every day like he was making a million dollars," said former player Cliff Godwin, who is now the ECU head coach. Soon Raleigh and Mazey left and Tommy Eason and Kevin McMullan had come in to join George and Keith. George was always the coach with the highest energy and the most potent motivational spark even though he was decades older than anyone else out on the field, said Erik Bakich, who played at ECU in 1999 and 2000 and is now the head baseball coach at the University of Michigan.

"He was just pure inspirational energy, outpacing everyone, constantly talking, constantly yelling, going at 100 percent," Bakich said. "Nobody gets more fired up than Coach Whit. He would call everyone 'stud', but he was the biggest stud of anyone."

George jumped right into the Pirate Nation, determined to help his alma mater become a national baseball power and fulfill the objective LeClair stated when he was hired: Qualification for the College World Series in Omaha. Division I baseball was another world from the fields at Richmond Senior High or Pitt Community College, but the fundamentals of the game were the same, and the priorities of a team that wanted to have success—hard work, relentless conditioning and mental toughness—transcended the differences in budgets, stadium size or media spotlight.

At practice George was a bundle of energy, never content just to sit and watch events unfold but always quick to jump up and hit fungoes or stride out to the outfield to help a player with a defensive stance, said Nick Schnabel, another Pirate player from that era who now works with Bakich at Michigan as an assistant coach. "He was always looking to do something," Schnabel said. "If I had a nickel for every ground ball he had hit me in two years, I'd be a rich man. Always, always, looking for something to do and to help guys get better. Always. He had more energy than anybody on the field, and that went for practice, that went for games. There was no off switch."

The timing of George's arrival at ECU couldn't have been better for Cory Scott, who had played on his first Pitt Community College team and considers him one of his most influential mentors. After playing at PCC for two years, Scott's dream was to finish his college career at ECU, but as his sophomore spring semester ended his grades were too low to make the switch to Division I. George and Keith asked him to come to ECU to talk about it, and there they told him that he could have a spot on the Pirates squad if he worked hard to boost his grades over the summer.

"Coach Whit called me in and told me he was never going to give up on me, that my next step was East Carolina," Scott said. "Both of them said, "You get your grades up this summer, Bud, you've got a spot on our team. And I worked hard and I got on the team, and Coach Whit was there. He was always so proud of me, because I was his."

In 1998, George's first year as an ECU assistant, the Pirates finished 30-29 as the staff tweaked the roster to fit their philosophy. In one disappointing game on the road at

Richmond, the Pirates held a sturdy lead but let the Spiders come back to beat them. Keith's postgame dressing down of the players is one moment from that maiden season that stands out in George's mind. "I never heard Keith use a bad word, but that one time," he said. "We were down in right field and Keith looked at the guys and said, 'It's a hell of a note when you've got a coach who's seventy-some years old who's got more enthusiasm than you guys have got."

In their next season, with the new "Omaha-or-bust" philosophy firmly established and the kind of grueling early-morning workouts that made George proud standard practice, the Pirates finished the season 46-16 with top 25 rankings in three national polls. Their success earned them a trip to the NCAA Regional in Baton Rouge, where they won their first two games before falling to top-seed and tournament host LSU. The 2000 squad finished 47-13 and won the Colonial Athletic Association title in its last year in that conference before moving to Conference USA, setting the Pirates up for a 2001 season that brought them closer to Omaha than they had ever been.

Keith and George, while three decades apart in age, were cut from the same coaching cloth. That was illustrated vividly one day in 1999, when a player named Lee Delfino, who had been a highly touted recruit from Canada, showed up at practice late. Coach LeClair stopped everything and told Delfino to start running, and after some initial resistance he put on his turf shoes and did just that. Delfino ran from foul pole to foul pole, across the outfield, for the entirety of practice, then a few months later hit a home run over the fence to defeat a legendary LSU team at the NCAA Regional. His words to Keith, right before he hit the bomb, were, "I'm going to end this thing."

"He came up and he hit a home run, and when he turned at third base, he looked at Keith and he said, 'This one's for you, coach.' And I'll never forget that."

With his non-stop energy and enthusiasm, George helped fuel the Pirates as they developed a habit of winning near the end of the century. Always a big believer in the sweeping motivational gesture, George's pregame tour de force came before the 2000 season-ending series against UNC-Wilmington, remembers Cliff Godwin, who played for ECU from 1998 to 2002 and became the Pirates head coach in 2015. The Pirates had to sweep the Seahawks for a share of the regular season conference championship, and George was determined to get them fired up in a most memorable way.

"Coach Whit got the biggest jockstrap I had ever seen," Godwin said. "And when I say the biggest jockstrap, it was like as big as a person. I don't even know where he got it. He said, 'You boys, we're going to go in there, we're going to kick their ass this weekend, and guys that are really tough and fight for the weekend, we're going to put their name on this jockstrap.' So at the end of the weekend, he had the jockstrap filled up with players names written in Sharpie. And we swept UNCW, and we were co-conference champs."

The 2001 squad went undefeated in its NCAA Regional, setting up a Super Regional against Tennessee at Grainger Stadium in none other than George's hometown of Kinston, which was serving as ECU's de facto home field since they were the host team of the tournament. In a heartbreaking series that would eventually be remembered for much more than baseball, the Pirates fell in two games to the Volunteers and dashed the very real Omaha hopes of the Pirate Nation. But when George and all of Keith LeClair's former players recall that weekend, they think only of the fact that it was their last "normal" time together as a team, their last game before learning the devastating news that LeClair, only thirty-six, had ALS.

Through LeClair's shattering diagnosis and quick physical decline George became a rock, both for the Pirate baseball family and the LeClair family. He visited Keith regularly throughout a 2002 season in which Keith remained the head coach but struggled with speech and mobility until eventually, early that spring, he had to stop sitting in the dugout during games altogether. George teamed with Eason and McMullan to keep the baseball routine going while trying to provide emotional support for young men who were worried about their coach's health.

For George and his fellow Pirates, all of the emotions of that 2002 season converged at the Conference USA Tournament, which was held in Kinston in May. Keith's support team had rigged up a special van with a recliner and parked it right outside the fence adjacent to right field at Grainger Stadium. From that vantage point, he got to watch his team, new members of the larger conference and the sixth seed in the tournament, dispatch one opponent after another and win the C-USA title. As they took down first TCU, then South Florida, then the top-seeded University of Houston, Whitfield marveled at what he was seeing from a team that had endured so much. "Every single time that Houston mounted any kind of rally, we'd have something spectacular happen," he said of that final game. "And the last time it happened, I turned to Mac (assistant coach Kevin McMullan) and said, 'We've got a tenth player out there today.' We were doing things that were unbelievable."

When that victory over the Cougars was sealed, winning pitcher Davey Penny grabbed a cooler full of Gatorade and started toward the van as every other Pirate player followed. They poured the Gatorade over the front of the van and then lined up at the side door to congratulate their coach who had been forced to go on a ventilator to breathe just a month before. For George and so many others who love and follow the Diamond Bucs, that unlikely victory and the amazing gesture that followed it became the most indelible symbol of Keith's courageous fight against a debilitating disease.

When Keith stepped down as head coach after that 2002 season and former ECU assistant Randy Mazey took over, George decided it was the right time for him to finally retire. His time with Keith and the players in that group was so special that he knew better than to stay and try to replicate it. He keeps in touch with many of the players from those years, and he has watched with pride as they have taken the lessons about toughness, leadership and character in Greenville and passed them on to other young men in every part of the country. As of 2021 the LeClair coaching tree had produced two Division I head baseball coaches and five Division I and major league assistants or scouts. Whenever possible, the coaches wear the number 23 in memory of LeClair, who died of ALS in 2006.

"I'm not sure that we'll ever have a group as close as that group was at East Carolina," George said. "I don't know whether we'll ever have that again, because it was a sort of once-in-a-lifetime. They were close from the first day to the last day, as long as they played. And they still correspond with each other every week; everybody knows what everybody's doing. And it's so neat to me that all of 'em are wearing 23."

In the final years of Keith's life, when George had more free time because he had retired from coaching at ECU, he went over to Keith's house to visit him nearly every day, always talking baseball and faith. Keith lost his ability to speak early in his illness, so he communicated through a special "Eye Gaze" computer that allowed him to look at letters and, using only his eyes, type words that were then broadcast through the speaker. He also used the Eye Gaze to write Christian devotionals that he e-mailed out to family and friends, who subsequently shared them with untold numbers of people. Some of George's most treasured times are sitting quietly with Keith and his family or taking part in the Bible study at Keith's house with coaches like former ECU track coach Bill Carson, longtime

ECU administrator Henry Van Sant and others who joined in when they could.

George was finally in retirement mode, and the lack of coaching responsibilities gave him more freedom to travel to sporting events, especially major league baseball games and the College World Series. Whether he was actively coaching the sport or not, baseball was still his main hobby and passion, although he carved out plenty of time to watch other sports as well. He traveled with friends, planned his clinic and hall of fame each January, ate plenty of barbecue and steak dinners and enjoyed his children and grandchildren. He figured out a way to do retirement in his own high-energy style and would have been content to stay in that routine, but to his surprise, in late 2005, he learned that his time at ECU was not quite finished.

Randy Mazey had left the head coaching post abruptly in October, putting his former assistant Billy Godwin in the top job with little time to prepare for the 2006 season. Billy and George had a long friendship dating back to Billy's annual pilgrimage to the Richmond County baseball clinic when he was a young baseball prospect. Then in the 1990s, the two had coached against each other in American Legion ball – George back in Goldsboro and Billy in Rocky Mount. So when he suddenly found himself at the helm of Pirate baseball, Billy knew exactly who he needed to add to his staff to help him transition into his first Division I head coaching gig. Like Keith LeClair had eight years earlier, he picked up the phone and dialed George's number.

"It was a tough time of the year, being in October, to hire a staff, and I felt like he was the perfect fit, and I mean that in more ways than one," Billy Godwin said. "Knew East Carolina, loved East Carolina. Certainly well-respected, knowledgeable, somebody I trusted to come in and help me for the year."

In 2020 Link Jarrett became the head baseball coach at Notre Dame, but in 2006 he was a newly hired assistant coach at ECU, working alongside George. A Florida native who played at Florida State, Jarrett was unfamiliar with George's considerable legacy when he arrived in Greenville. His first impression of the seasoned coach was a memorable one: The Pirates were ranked sixth in the conference in preseason polls, and George addressed the team about that prediction with his usual inspirational flair.

"I didn't know enough about Conference USA to know if that's where we belonged or not," Jarrett said. "But we had our first team meeting and George stood up and he said, 'I'll tell you this. Being picked sixth in Conference USA is a slap in the face.' And he hauled off and slapped himself in the face, hard. I about fell out of my chair."

But it wasn't long before Jarrett considered George one of his most important influences in baseball and beyond. The foundation of that friendship was Link's willingness to explore Eastern N.C. lunch spots with George, an expert on barbecue and country cooking establishments. "Frequently he would walk into my office, and he would say, 'Stud, you ever had some barbecue? Get in the car.' And he would put me in the car, and off we'd go, we would talk about baseball and life.' We went to Bum's, Strickland Dail, all kinds of places. Those rides with him, we would go forty-five minutes sometimes, and I loved every minute of it."

The 2006 squad finished 33-26 and (regrettably to all, but especially to George) the predicted sixth in Conference USA. But George's presence helped Billy and his staff find their footing en route to three consecutive NCAA Regional trips in 2007, 2008 and 2009. "He coached the outfielders for us, and it was amazing, with all the experience he's had as a head coach, how he took to that role as an assistant," Billy said. "He was somebody that people trusted and respected, and I thought he was the perfect fit for the situation we were in."

When that season had concluded, George did settle into a longer chapter of retirement, with one more surprise still in store. The lasting imprints of two different stints as an ECU assistant coach were the relationships with the players and coaches there, and his time as a Diamond Buc coach also served to strengthen his stake in the team's success. He had always followed Pirate baseball as an alumnus, but his experience there since 1997 has made him not just a friend but a confidant for administrators and coaches. When Cliff Godwin took the head coaching job in Greenville, George was able to continue a relationship whose roots went back to Cliff's Pirate playing career, and Cliff's respect and appreciation for his former coach has only grown.

"You see the competitive side of him, and then get to know Coach Whit as I have over the years, you see the compassionate side, and how much he cares for his former players," Cliff Godwin said. "He's still coming up to the ECU baseball office, and he gives all the coaching staff chocolate-covered almonds for Christmas. Really the servant leadership he lives on a day-to-day basis, just giving back to people, is pretty impressive."

As much as his rooting interest in ECU has intensified in the past fifteen years, so too has George's following of the teams where former Pirate stars are now setting the lineups, whether it's Michigan (Erik Bakich and Nick Schnabel), Notre Dame (Link Jarrett), UCLA (Bryant Ward), or the Los Angeles Dodgers (Clayton McCullough). In fact, when Michigan defeated UCLA in the NCAA Super Regional to qualify for the College World Series in Omaha in 2019, the staff had not even returned to their office in Ann Arbor yet before George had called informing the Wolverines baseball secretary of his intention to be at the College World Series to cheer them on.

He was there, in his favorite seat behind home plate, when Bakich and Schnabel's team finished as national runner-up. And it isn't just his former players and coaching colleagues he tracks; in some cases, George now has a second generation of ballplayers deserving of his attention, like Link Jarrett's son J.T., who joined the N.C. State team in 2018. Whenever Link is in town to watch J.T., he tries to gather up other Wolfpack parents and take them to the Beefmastor, a legendary steak restaurant in Wilson that he was introduced to years earlier by his friend and noted steak-lover George Whitfield.

"He's just a remarkable man in every sense of the word," Jarrett said. "It's not just baseball. Baseball brought us together, but that is just a piece of what I cherish about George. It's not all baseball, not all coaching, it's just him and his character and his stories and his passion for everything in this world."

CHAPTER 10

On the Road

By the summer of 2006, George had fully settled into the retirement life, which meant something quite different for him than it does for the majority of senior Americans looking for a relaxed, sedentary lifestyle. After coaching his final game for East Carolina, he pivoted his attention to traveling to sporting events, connecting with family, friends and former players and keeping up with baseball—especially the teams which featured former players or their children coaching or playing.

Anyone who knows George well knows that inactivity doesn't suit him well at all, so he turned his boundless energy to the pursuit of sports opportunities. He became a superfan for his hometown Kinston High School, where his friend and head basketball coach Wells Gulledge was building a juggernaut that won three state basketball championships in five years. Each winter he would watch the Vikings in the state tournament, and then take them out to dinner, win or lose. "He has fed more kids and done more for kids and communities than anybody will ever know," Gulledge said.

George is the patron saint of the adage, "All you have to do is ask," and over and over, during and after his coaching career, he proved that extraordinary doors can open to you when you aren't afraid to make an inquiry of the gatekeeper. "For some unknown reason, I've never been afraid to ask anybody for anything," he said. "I just call them up."

Consider George's presence at one of the most seminal college basketball games in the history of his state – N.C. State's national championship victory over the University of Houston in 1983. Immortalized by the ESPN 30 For 30 "Survive and Advance" and the image of Wolfpack coach Jim Valvano running around the University of New Mexico arena floor looking for someone to hug, it's typical of George's Forrest Gump-like presence at big events that he was right there that night, sitting courtside, when Lorenzo Charles caught Dereck Whittenburg's off-kilter shot and turned it into an alley-oop basket to seal the title for N.C. State's Cinderella team.

That particular adventure started at Richmond Senior High School, where George was working as athletic director in the spring of 1983. He had met N.C. State's young magnetic head coach Jim Valvano through his friend Sam Esposito, the Wolfpack head baseball coach, and he was impressed with Valvano's approach to leading his team and his zest for life. When N.C. State marched improbably through its NCAA Tournament opponents one nail-biter at a time and punched its ticket to the final four in Albuquerque, George couldn't get one thought out of his mind: He wanted to be there. "I was in my office at the end of a PE class, thinking to myself, God knows I'd give a million dollars to see State win this game, 'cause I loved Valvano," George said. "I picked up the telephone and called Coach Esposito, who had several of my players on scholarship."

"George! How are ya doing!" Esposito asked.

"Coach, I'm gonna ask you something I know you can't do," George replied. "I'd give my right arm to go see State play down in Albuquerque."

"Pack your bags, be here at 12:00 tomorrow. I'll put you on the bus with the cheerleaders and the band and you can fly on the plane with them."

Twenty-four hours later, George was part of the traveling party heading to the Final Four with a Wolfpack team that will endure forever in college basketball lore. Not only did he fly to the game with the cheerleaders and the band, George had front-row seats to that wild finish between the Wolfpack and the Cougars. And when N.C. State had sealed the trophy, George was among the people, like Valvano, running around celebrating on the floor. "When the buzzer went off, I ran onto the court just like Valvano!" George said. "It was crazy. Everybody was cheering and jumping up and down. I've got that 30 For 30 right down there and I cry every time I see it. Every time that I see that I remember the feeling that he had with those players."

George has beaten a path to big-time sporting events repeatedly using a number of different connections, but more often than not the door is opened by a former player whose hard work and talent landed him in the big time. In 1977 Louis Breeden, who had played for George on the Hamlet Post 49 team in 1972, was drafted by the Cincinnati Bengals. In 1982, when the Bengals and Breeden competed in Super Bowl XVI against the San Francisco 49ers in the Pontiac Silverdome, George was there to experience the milestone in person.

That was George's only Super Bowl trip (so far), but he has attended the World Series six times, twice to cheer on his former Richmond County players – in 1988 to see Franklin Stubbs compete for the world champion Dodgers and in 1997 to see Alvin Morman pitch for the Indians against the Marlins. He has been to the Final Four five times, the College World Series in Omaha fourteen times, often to see former players, and MLB spring training and the Army-Navy game many times. Suffice it to say that the walls of George's Goldsboro home, full as they are of pictures from unforgettable sports outings and dozens of signed baseballs, would inspire plenty of envy in the average sports fan.

The paths of George's "boys" are so expansive within the world of professional sports that at times they have even faced off against each other. One of his favorite experiences, and an extraordinary coincidence by any measure, happened on September 27, 1999 in Detroit. George was there to witness the last game played in Tiger Stadium before the team moved into its new stadium, Comerica Park. That evening, improbably, pitchers for each team – Alvin Morman for the Royals and Brian Moehler for the Tigers — were both George's "boys," former Richmond County athletes who played on his Hamlet American Legion team within five years of one another.

Of course, all of these adventures happened when George was still working, either in high school coaching or administration or at the college level, so after he retired in 2006 he found himself even more free to check schedules and plan his calendar around the sporting events he most wanted to witness. Two years after he left ECU and twenty-five years after seeing college basketball history made firsthand in Albuquerque, George went to an auction to support a young player and found himself in another one of those situations that make his friends shake their heads in wonder.

Tanner Biagini, a talented member of the D.H. Conley team that won two consecutive state championships, had gone on to play at Virginia Military Institute – a college opportunity facilitated in part by George's connections with top VMI supporters. In 2008, when Biagini was a sophomore, he invited George to come to Richmond for a charity auction benefiting the athletic department. George knew that the auction would include a variety of keepsakes and beach and mountain vacations, but when he walked into the room and perused the table he saw something that interested him more – an opportunity to bid on a VMI basketball road trip. The winner would accompany the VMI Keydets squad when they took on the University of Kentucky in Rupp Arena on November 14. George quickly put in a bid for $25.

George had never seen a game at Rupp and he had long aspired to, so he stayed close by that table as the night wore on, trading bids with another man and eventually upping the ante to $250. His opponent, who had been slipping off to the bar intermittently to refresh his bourbon, had gotten to know George through the process and finally told him, "Look, I've gotta have another bourbon, so I'm going over to get a drink. And you stand right here, and if nobody else bids, I'll let you have this."

So George would have his trip to Rupp Arena, and VMI coach Duggar Baucom said he could bring his son Gef along. That would have been enough, but instead, in typical George fashion, he was sitting at the end of the VMI bench for the most seismic victory in the school's history. In front of 25,443 Kentucky fans, with George and Gef getting the royal treatment all evening as if they were part of the VMI staff, the Keydets toppled the Wildcats 111-103. A decade later, it was still the last time Kentucky had been defeated by a non-Power Five team.

"The VMI coach said, 'Boys, we're the only ones in this whole arena that think we can win tonight, but I'll tell you why we're gonna win. When you cross midcourt, don't hesitate. I will not say a word to you. If you see an open shot let it fly,'" George said. "They hit ten straight frees and jumped out to a huge lead. In the last two minutes of the game, Kentucky caught up at 103-103 and VMI shot the last eight free throws and won the game 111-103. They went crazy."

As far as Baucom and his team were concerned, George and Gef had played the part of talisman. When they returned to Lexington, Va. on the bus, the Whitfields were in a time crunch because they had to go straight to Durham for George's son-in-law's master's program graduation. George asked someone from the team if the bus could be moved, because it was blocking his car, but he was told, "No Coach, first you've got to come in the locker room!" He and Gef went in and were surrounded by the players, who thanked them and gave them a VMI jersey signed by every member of the team. "I never thought it would be that great," George said. "I never thought it would turn into something like that. For $250."

If there's a good seat to be had or a personal connection to be made that leads to a better view, expect George to find it, his friends have learned. Tate Mooring has accompanied George to Omaha for the College World Series five times, and while the whole experience is unforgettable, two aspects stand out: The Omaha steaks they eat for virtually every meal and George's regular seats right behind home plate. George, and friends like Tate who are lucky enough to join him in Omaha, are clearly visible in every television shot of the batter, and with thousands of friends and former players tuning in George is peppered with constant phone calls from friends who catch a glimpse of him. Eventually as the innings progress, George's cell phone usually dies, Tate said, and then they can focus exclusively on the game.

Scott Altman, a former Hamlet American Legion player, remembers being surprised the first time he thought he saw his old coach on TV during the College World Series broadcast, and because the camera moved around quickly he couldn't be sure he was looking at Coach Whitfield. He called his brother Heath, another one of George's "boys," and asked him if he saw George there to the left of the plate. Heath told Scott that he would call George to investigate. "I'm watching TV, and I see Whitfield answer the phone," Scott Altman said. "I know who he's talking to."

Reid Parrott and Claude Kennedy are two of George's oldest friends from their growing-up years in Kinston, and they have also been companions on countless sports tourism adventures. George's uncanny gift for talking people into things, or even just having upgrades like first-class airplane seats or choice stadium tickets improbably handed to him, has become almost commonplace to them. Claude was George's companion at the 1997 World Series between the Indians (featuring former Richmond County standout Alvin Morman) and the Marlins. When the two men arrived at the stadium on a cold Cleveland night, they discovered that their seats were in the chilly upper deck and their view of the field was far from optimal. For the first five innings, they found a concrete landing with better access to the field, and they moved back and forth between the landing and their seats to get a better look at the action. But then they walked into the concourse and struck up a conversation with a security officer who was guarding the entrance to the park's luxury boxes and restaurant.

"It was the coldest night I've ever seen in my life," George said. "The wind was whirling, so we went down and they had a big lounge thing, where all the big people were, and we knocked on the door. And the policemen came to the door and we said, "Is there any way we could get in here?"

"No sir," the guard said. "These are all people that are season ticket holders and big people with the Cleveland Indians. Where are you guys from?"

"We're from Kinston, North Carolina."

"I was in the service in North Carolina. I was down at Camp Lejeune."

George and the guard kept chatting, and soon he opened the door and let them into the restaurant, where they watched the rest of the game in warmth and comfort. Before they left, the guard found out that they had tickets for the next night's game as well, so he told them that even though he wasn't working they just had to go find a certain guard and they would be allowed into the luxury suite again. So they traded biting wind and obstructed views for a considerably upgraded viewing experience, which is the kind of serendipitous occurrence that Claude and Reid connect to going places with their old friend. "George has a knack," Claude said. George is known to call his old friends with just hours to spare with an impulsive plan to drive to a game or to an out-of-town restaurant for a good steak, but even if the calls seem abrupt Reid and Claude almost always say yes. They're afraid of what they might miss if they don't.

Bud Andrews, who played for George in Goldsboro in the '60s, has also been fortunate enough to travel with his former coach to an array of interesting sporting events, from the Preakness to the Army-Navy game, which George has attended eighteen times. Like Claude and Reid, he has been the beneficiary of upgrades brought about by George's persuasive, friendly demeanor and his myriad connections. One time the men, along with one of Bud's friends, went to a Baltimore Orioles game in the evening after spending all day at the Preakness, and George managed to get them some of the best seats in the park at the last minute. That was also the day that Andrews was reminded that his friend doesn't just love the sport of baseball; he has forgotten more about it than most people ever knew.

The trio was watching the game from their choice seats and George made a prediction about how the Orioles, who were batting, would advance the score. "Boys, I wouldn't be surprised if they do a suicide squeeze here," Andrews recalled him saying. Sure enough, Baltimore executed a suicide squeeze on its next play, getting the runner home. Andrews turned to him, a bit amazed, and asked, "How did you know that?" George responded, "A year or so ago in Florida, they had the same guy at the plate in a similar situation. He squeezed him then, I figured they'd squeeze him now."

Most of George's trips, whether spontaneous or planned long in advance, revolve around sporting events, but he has a few other passions that can prompt him to make travel arrangements. He has always loved country music, particularly old classic country, and he never turns down a chance to go watch favorite artists perform. He has also had the chance to visit the Country Music Hall of Fame, and when his former player Velton Ray Bunch offered him the opportunity to meet one of his musical heroes, he was all in. Dolly Parton was coming to Charlotte, and Bunch was able to pull strings to not only get George tickets to the show, but access backstage afterwards so that he could meet Dolly. "He was on cloud nine," Bunch said. "It was great."

While former players and friends were often his traveling companions, or even the facilitators, of George's many adventures, no friendship opened as many doors as the one he enjoyed with Clyde King. Through Clyde's distinguished career in professional baseball – as manager or coach with five different clubs and most notably with the Yankees in the '70s and '80s – he arranged for countless baseball games, spring training trips and meetings with baseball royalty for his old friend George. Starting when Clyde invited George's first Hamlet team to catch a game when he was the pitching coach in Pittsburgh and they met the great Roberto Clemente, all the way to their last trip to Yankee Stadium together shortly before Clyde's death in 2010, when they sat in George Steinbrenner's box and Yogi Berra came by to say hi, the two Eastern North Carolina men experienced quite a bit together.

That Yankee Stadium trip was facilitated by another faithful friend of George's, Gil Minor from Richmond, Va. The two met through Clyde, and Gil flew them up to New York on his company's private jet. The most memorable part of the series, Gil said, was when Berra walked into the box and George disappeared, reappearing a few minutes later with baseballs from the souvenir stand that the friends could have Berra sign. "He became Clyde's eyes and ears," said Minor, who supports George's baseball clinic every year and talks to him on the phone weekly. "He took him everywhere he wanted to go."

"They had a friendship that was just phenomenal, and I can say with a great deal of certainty that Clyde looked at George as a son," said Johnny Peacock, who is married to Clyde's youngest daughter Janet. "There was just something special about George that Clyde would never say no to. Clyde opened up a lot of doors for George, but vice versa was true too. Clyde always had incredible respect for George."

When Clyde, who was twelve years older than George, found himself unable to drive long distances as he grew older, it was George who became his de facto chauffeur, and the adventures continued. One Friday, Clyde called George and asked if he could drive him to Grandfather Mountain the next day for a lunch gathering. Even though it's clear across the state, George agreed, and he showed up at Clyde's house early the next morning. They arrived at Grandfather Golf and Country Club and were greeted by Hugh Morton, the legendary photographer and owner of the community, but George still didn't know exactly what he was walking into. Morton escorted them to a back dining room and they found their seat at the table.

"A few minutes passed, then a guy walks in the door and says, 'Hi, I'm Don Shula,'" George said. The next person walks up, 'I'm Bob Griese.' Then, 'I'm Paul Dietzel, LSU Bengal Tigers.' Mack Brown had a place up there, and he was there too. They all played golf up there, and Hugh Morton had them up there every spring and they would get together and play golf and they'd all eat lunch together."

It was exactly the sort of surprise that George relished, since he dearly loved meeting sports figures and hearing their stories. He left that day with a football signed by Shula and Griese, the coach and quarterback for the undefeated 1972 Miami Dolphins, and Dietzel, the former head football coach and athletic director at LSU. Just another piece of memorabilia signaling an eventful day with Clyde, and a companion to his three-story case of baseballs signed by the likes of Brooks Robinson, Stan Musial, Ted Williams, Tommy John, Bobby Richardson, Pee Wee Reese, Sandy Koufax, Al Kaline, Bob Feller, Carleton Fisk, Trot Nixon, and Tommy LaSorda. "Every one of them, I got them personally to sign it," George said.

Any friend or former player who has ever traveled to an event with George has realized that he knows people everywhere, that it's nearly impossible to walk into any ballpark without hearing someone call "George!" or "Coach Whit!" and hustle up to greet him. Those in his inner circle like to talk about George's "two degrees of separation," pointing out that you can find your way from George to virtually anyone else in sports in just two steps. When Mark Johnson and George were working on the Mississippi State staff together in 1976, Johnson remembers that a bunch of guys were talking about spitting tobacco, and Mark said that he had played for a Mets minor league club with a guy who could spit with remarkable accuracy. When Mark said that the player's name was Rooster Narron, George exclaimed "Stop!" and explained that Rooster had been a star player for him on his Legion and Goldsboro High teams.

When he wasn't burning up the roads or the airways en route to another sports encounter, George was adding to his home memorabilia museum in a different way—by collecting accolades for his decades of coaching success at the high school and college level. In just one four-year period, he was named one of the 90 most influential people in N.C. high school sports history by the NCHSAA and inducted into the North Carolina Sports Hall of Fame (2005), the Kinston/Lenoir County Sports Hall of Fame (2007), and the North Carolina Baseball Coaches Association Hall of Fame (2008). He also received an Outstanding Alumni Award from the East Carolina Alumni Association in 2013, was recognized as one of the "100 Coaches to Remember" at the NCHSAA centennial celebration in 2014, and was inducted into the University of Mount Olive Athletics Hall of Fame, also in 2014. And in 2015 came an award from the Wilson Hot Stove League that tied his successes, his enduring friendship with Clyde, and their many shared experiences together; George was given the Clyde King Excellence in Coaching Award.

It was an exciting retirement marked by a series of milestones and adventures. When he was home in Goldsboro, he drove to Kinston often to watch his grandson Nicholas run cross-country at Arendell Parrott Academy. But at least one friend looked at George and saw something more than a grandfather enjoying his golden years; he saw an opportunity for a coach's perfect curtain call.

CHAPTER 11

One More Mountain

Dr. Bert Bright was a teacher and football coach at Parrott Academy in Kinston when he met one of the city's favorite sons out on the football field. George Whitfield liked to stop by Parrott to watch football practice, and the two coaches invariably found each other to swap stories and strategies. As their friendship grew, Bright learned more about Whitfield's matchless coaching career, and before long Bright was promoted to the job of headmaster at Parrott.

In the summer of 2014, the school was looking for a baseball coach, and that job opening started the wheels turning in Bright's mind: A legendary and proven coach was right under their nose at Parrott, attending games and practices and dropping by Bright's office regularly to visit. The next time he stopped by, Bright jumped into the deep end.

"I said 'George, what do you think about putting those baseball cleats on one more time?'" Bright recalled. "And he looked at me and rolled his eyes and he just kind of laughed." George left that day and went home, back into a retirement lifestyle that was busy and fulfilling, but still he fixated on Bright's question. He had loved his years as an ECU assistant coach in his final decade of coaching, but he hadn't had the chance to be a head coach since 1995, twenty years earlier. Should he embrace one more opportunity, back at the high school level that had been so good to him for so many years in Goldsboro and Richmond County?

Once the idea was planted, it started to take root for George. He certainly had not been seeking another coaching opportunity, but his friend Wells Gulledge was the basketball coach at Parrott, he liked the idea of being a part of his grandson's school and coaching drew him for the same reasons it always had: The relationships with the boys and the chance to help them achieve something great as a team. A day or two later, he was back at the school, and he casually stuck his head into Bright's office door.

"Were you serious about that offer?" George asked.

"Absolutely, I'm serious about that offer. Let's talk about it."

"Everybody's going to think you're crazy, hiring a seventy-nine-year-old coach."

Bright assured George that he knew what he was doing, and soon Parrott had its coach and George had his final team. That agreement between two friends set the stage for a career encore performance that seemed too much like fiction to be real-life. In fact, as Bright put it, "You could do a movie just on that year."

Tate Mooring first encountered George in 2005 when they were in the same group traveling to the basketball Final Four in St. Louis. A former Parrott baseball player, he looked up to George and loved to hear the stories he told when they met in Mooring's hometown of La Grange at George's favorite restaurant there, Ken's Grill. One day they were enjoying a sandwich when Tate brought up the fact that his alma mater was hunting for a baseball coach, oblivious to the fact that he was on the same trail as the Parrott headmaster.

"I kind of just mentioned one time, I played at Parrott Academy, and we're looking for a baseball coach. I think it would be really cool to have a coach like you out there one day," Mooring said. "He didn't laugh, he didn't do much, he just kind of gritted his teeth and kind of smirked. And a few weeks later I got a phone call from him and he said, 'I wanted to talk to you about the Parrott Academy baseball job.'"

After George asked Tate for his perspective on the position, he asked him if he would be willing to come serve as one of his assistant coaches, giving Tate the chance to play a supporting role in the dramatic events that would follow. "He said, 'Would you help me?' I answered so quickly, because George Whitfield asked me. It wasn't going to be a 'no.' Whatever came out of his mouth, a 'yes' was going to come out of mine."

Word got out quickly in Kinston: George Whitfield was coaching baseball again in his hometown. The Patriot players had been born around the time George was helping Keith LeClair at East Carolina, and even if they didn't remember his accomplishments they soon started hearing bits and pieces about their new coach. Zaccheus Rasberry, an APA junior at the time, heard enough to make him a bit nervous. He heard that George had attended The Citadel, so he ran his practices like military drills. He heard that anytime his teams did anything wrong, they had to run. "It was a little bit intimidating, but just based off of all the things he's done, it's kind of like, 'Well, if his teams are winning, he must be doing something right,'" said Rasberry, who went on to play baseball for Louisburg College and Presbyterian College.

The first day of school was still weeks away when George took the job, but he asked Dr. Bright for the players' contact information so that he could reach out and get to know them. These young men might have been engaged with social media platforms that George had never heard of, but they had more commonalities with his Goldsboro and Richmond County players of decades ago than they had differences. "The first thing you've got to learn is you've got to learn the kids," he told the Kinston Free-Press that June. "You've got to learn what makes them tick."

Friends of George's, fellow old-school coaches and others from his generation, warned him that he might find these children of the 2000s harder to motivate than his players from the '60s, '70s and '80s. Kids of that age were distracted by cellphones and prone to quit when things got hard, he was told, and they wouldn't respond to strict coaching standards and outfield sprints like their predecessors had. When he told some people at Parrott that he intended to enter his new team in an Easter tournament to expose them to some challenging opponents, he heard warnings that Parrott families always took vacations over Spring Break and the kids wouldn't be willing to sacrifice their trips for baseball.

So as soon as he could gather the boys, he broached the subject as only George can. "I said to them, 'Fellas, if we want to get better, we need to play some good teams. We've been asked to participate in a tournament over in Wilson, and there are going to be thirty-some teams in this tournament; a lot of them are Class 4A teams. I want to know if you guys are committed to play in the Easter tournament.' I said, 'Don't tell me right now. I want you go to home tonight, and you tell your parents what I'm saying. If push comes to shove and they're going to go and you have to stay, you can stay with me.'

"They came back the next day and every single one of them said, 'We're staying. We want to play.'"

To be on the Parrott athletic staff with George was a dream for Gulledge, who had literally been a friend of the Whitfield family's since birth. A native of Hamlet, Wells grew up down the street from George and, even though he didn't play baseball, admired his prolific success as a coach in his home county. When he was approaching his graduation from Richmond Senior High and thinking about playing college basketball, Wells signed with Mount Olive College, in large part because his mentor George had become the athletic director there the previous year. Now a high school basketball coach at Ashley High in Wilmington with three state titles of his own from his time at Kinston High School, Wells has never made a career move without first consulting George.

The fall of 2014 found both of the men serving as head coaches at Parrott – Wells for basketball and George for baseball, but they also worked together as assistant football coaches. Wells made it one of his chief duties to get his seventy-nine-year-old friend to exercise some caution on the football field, especially after George climbed onto a tackling sled in practice one day and was thrown off by some hard-hitting linemen. The accident severely injured George's wrist, Wells said, but he stayed for the duration of practice. That same season, the Patriots were playing at Hobgood Academy when a player barreled over the sideline and flattened George, knocking him out cold for several minutes. "That's as scared as I've ever been," Wells said.

When baseball practice started early in 2015, Coach Whit, as the boys knew him then, didn't run them as hard as they had feared, although he made it clear that his expectations were high and that they had joined a long line of baseball players who had achieved greatness because they worked harder and believed in themselves more fervently than the team in the other dugout. Every day at the beginning of practice, before they took batting practice or infield, George gathered the Patriots on the bleachers and told them about a former player who had beaten the odds, or of a team that had made it much further than they had a right to. Mooring called them George's "life stories and life lessons," and they were an integral part of the Coach Whit training program.

"I can't even imagine playing for him in his earlier days, from what I've heard," said Connor Bright, who was a freshman on that team and signed with the Air Force Academy after graduating from APA. "He was definitely a little bit more mellow with us, but Coach Whit is Coach Whit, he's going to be fiery, and he's going to yell and run us and stuff like that. That's just his style, he loves to motivate us. He stayed true to that as best he could."

The players, parents and fans all knew that the 2015 Parrott Academy Patriots had plenty of talent, that if any team could make it a long way in the NC Independent Schools Athletic Association 2A schedule it would be them. And when George took the helm, the expectations rose even more. Until the season started in early March and they lost two of their first three games by large margins. "It wasn't necessarily the best start to the season, but then things went on and we kind of figured things out and came together as a team," Rasberry said. "We were able to beat some bigger schools, even public 4A schools that a lot of people didn't see us competing with. Just with everything coach was telling us to do, whether it was running or just a little short story before practice, it was something that was going to benefit us in the long run."

George and the players didn't panic; he kept drilling them in fundamentals and field vision every afternoon, kept reminding them what hard work could bring them and kept telling them stories about athletes who had overcome rocky starts and steep odds. The way the young men rallied confirmed what he believed: The life of teenagers might look quite different, but at their core young people respond when someone sees the potential for greatness within them and pushes them to fulfill it.

"They were great kids to coach and they worked hard," he said. "They ran just as hard as any team I had. I found out this and I believe this with all my heart: times have definitely changed, and kids have changed, because they've got more things to do than when I first started. But if they're inspired enough and you give them something to work for, and they really want it bad enough, they'll go after it. I believe that."

After suffering one more loss on March 13, the Patriots won the next nine games and fourteen out of the next sixteen. One highlight for Rasberry and his teammates was that Easter tournament in Wilson, when the Patriots defeated the 3A Hunt High School 9-8. After also defeating larger schools Southern Nash and Nash Central Parrott won that tournament, and it marked a turning point for the team, George recalled, serving as evidence that they could go toe-to-toe with anyone they might face in the postseason.

"From that day on, they thought they were pretty good," George said. "And I tried not to tell them any different."

The Patriots entered the state tournament full of confidence, but in the semifinal game against Rocky Mount Academy they fell behind and trailed by one in the ninth inning with two outs. It looked like the quest for the state title was over, and Connor Bright remembers trying to look on the bright side, telling himself that the team had a good run. "And then, from some sort of miracle, which was probably because Coach Whit was the coach, our player got a hit," he said. After the batter hit a single and stole second, Rasberry came up to bat and launched the ball to right field to score the winning run. "That was crazy," Connor Bright said. "We had talent, but it was definitely a lot of Cinderella things along the way."

After squeaking out that win, APA went on to face Harrells Christian Academy in the final best-of-three series. In a bit of symmetry that would thrill any scriptwriter, the setting for that state final was Grainger Stadium in Kinston, the minor league baseball park where George had played his own high school baseball, and also occasionally competed in his younger years. It was the place where a twelve-year-old George was standing in right field the only time his father was able to watch him play ball.

George and his Parrott players had spent the previous two months reinforcing their strengths and identifying and addressing their weaknesses with a tough schedule and demanding practices, so much so that by the time they played Harrells in the first game on May 15, 2015 the Patriots squad had all the tools they needed to check the last and most important box. They dispatched Harrells 6-4 that night, then came back the next night for a resounding 13-4 win that handed Parrott its second state title in history and its first in nearly twenty years. For Coach Whit, as those boys knew him, it was the fifth high school state title and the ninth overall including Legion championships, and he had improbably claimed state titles in four different decades. Mooring calls it "a miracle season."

"It was unbelievable," he said. "We had really good players. He had great talent, but the talent that we had, it needed Coach Whitfield. We had the talent to win many state championships, but that talent needed George Whitfield."

Throughout that season, George continued his tradition from earlier coaching gigs of taking his players out to eat, and he always insisted on picking up the bill. Dr. Bright, whose son Connor was on the team, and other parents tried to help with the meals but the coach always resisted. "George was like, "No, these are my boys," Bright said. But the week before the state championship game, Bright anticipated what was coming and got out ahead of George. He knew that George would take the team to a Kinston restaurant called The Baron and the Beef after the final game, win or lose, so he called the manager several days ahead of time and gave him a card number. "I was outside waiting for my son to come out, and George came out and you could tell he was fuming," Bright said.

As the Patriots carried out their triumphant run that spring, George weighed his options for the following school year. He felt energetic and healthy enough to coach again, but he was almost eighty and also knew that he could find plenty of good things to fill his time in the next phase of his retirement. Bright had known, when George took the job, that his time at Parrott would be brief, and the new trophy in the school's case guaranteed that it was memorable. So when Parrott hired a teacher with baseball coaching experience, he saw a clear path to leave with a successor in place. And besides, as his daughter Tyler reminded him, he wasn't likely to craft a better swan song to a baseball coaching career that had spanned fifty-six remarkable years.

George recalled: "My daughter said to me, 'Dad, don't you think it's about time to quit? I want you to think about something. The last game that you ever coached in your life was coached on the field where you played as a high school boy at Grainger Stadium. And you won a state championship in the place where you started. How much better could the Lord be to you than that?'"

Not only did that year give George a raft of new memories and another state title for his impressive collection, it expanded his network of "boys" to keep in contact with. He has kept close tabs on the college careers of players like Zaccheus Rasberry, Connor Bright, Charlie King (Davidson) and Colby McLawhorn (PCC), attending their games in person whenever possible, taking them out to eat when they're back in town and encouraging them over the phone through their season, always their coach. He is determined to make it to Connor's graduation from the Air Force Academy in 2022, because despite his abiding admiration of military heroes and his regular pilgrimage to the Army-Navy football game, he has never had the chance to see one of his "boys" graduate from a military academy.

"Every day with Coach Whit is pretty special," Connor said. "I think the main thing is just as a whole, Coach Whit will stop everything and make sure you're OK. He just really wants to provide every opportunity he can to everybody."

That new crop of "George's boys" had the opportunity to join a decades-long procession of others on August 21, 2016, when friends threw George an 80th birthday gala at the Goldsboro Event Center. George, who has an uncanny memory for numbers and stats, numbered the party guests at 394. As Larry Riggan put it, "I went to his 80th birthday party with 400 of his closest friends, and there were 400 who probably got left out." In the words of childhood buddy Alley Hart, "George has got more friends than anybody I know."

Dave Odom was the emcee for the festivities, and friends, former players and family members were given an opportunity to share tributes to George. One friend, Bob Kennel, who met George in the early '50s as his teammate on the Kinston American Legion team, read an original composition, a short poem called "The Ages of Mankind."

"George is one of my sports heroes," Kennel said. "He is absolutely a unique individual, and to still have the energy, intellect, commitment he has and to be such a beloved figure in his '80s, it's just amazing."

CHAPTER 12

Accolades

At Goldsboro Junior and Senior High Schools, Hamlet High and Richmond Senior, at Mount Olive, PCC, ECU and Parrott Academy, George had been known primarily for two things—coaching baseball and directing athletic programs. But through many of his working years and all of his various retirement phases, his dedication to his incomparable hall of fame and legendary baseball clinic ensured that he would also be known for the excitement he brings to dozens of families every January.

The honorees didn't used to number in the dozens; George's first group of inductees in 1985 included only three men, and all were esteemed college baseball coaches – Bill Wilhelm (Clemson), Jack Stallings (Wake Forest, Florida State and Georgia Southern) and Chuck Hartman (Virginia Tech). But as George's vision for the tradition grew and he had the opportunity to connect with a wider swath of people in athletics and beyond in recent decades, he expanded his list of honorees nearly every year. The class of thirty-one individuals he selected for 2021, which was postponed to 2022 because of the COVID-19 pandemic, would be his largest ever.

Raleigh tennis coach Steve Spivey in 2018, and the scores of others who proudly display their imposing plaques in their homes or offices, considered the selection to George's hall of fame an honor unlike any other—even if plenty of the men and women have been lauded by bodies with more name recognition than George's winter gathering in Goldsboro, N.C. Some have been elected to a half a dozen other halls of fame but value this one because they so respect the man who invited them. Others, particularly those who coached in sports or communities far from the spotlight, treasure their plaque and the memory of that night because they never expected to receive such recognition at all.

George's baseball clinic was born in 1972 when he was coaching at Hamlet High School. He was still young and had not made too many connections in the baseball world, but he knew that there was a world of knowledge about the game out there and that his small-town athletes would be better baseball players and men if they were exposed to some of it. "I was sitting in my office one afternoon before practice. And I told a couple of the other coaches, "I know our guys are probably tired of listening to us. Why don't we do something different, like maybe have a clinic and bring in some college coaches or some people to talk to our guys and have practice?' And they said, I think that's a great idea. So the first thing I did, I called Clyde. Clyde thought it was a great idea, too.'"

Pouncing on the plan with his characteristic enthusiasm, George started calling college baseball coaches and inviting them to come speak at the clinic, which was always held in January between the Christmas holidays and the commencement of high school and college baseball seasons. Coaches from every type of program would come, many year after year, proving George's former Mississippi State colleagues Ron Polk's and Mark Johnson 's point that it's nearly impossible to say 'no' to George. Every year he recruits coaches and solicits donations so that cost won't prohibit any young athlete from attending. His persistence has paid off; the consistent excellence and variety of instruction and George's careful planning of the weekend has given the clinic a reputation as one of the best in the nation.

"The unique thing about that is the fact that he brings so many kids into his clinic during that period that otherwise couldn't afford to go," said former Richmond County and MLB player Brian Moehler. "Because people will donate an admission and, really, you touch one kid, and that kid goes on to touch fifty kids down the road in his lifetime."

The clinic was originally targeted toward high school teams that travel there together for the day; George typically sends out about 250 flyers, one to the coach at every school within a hundred-mile radius of Goldsboro. But as the demands on teen athletes have grown and coaches have become less willing to ask their teams to make weekend commitments, George has expanded the registration to individual players as young as ten. When he started allowing individuals to sign up, he faced an attendant problem of supervision, so he created a provision that allowed each young man's father to attend for free with his son. Originally introduced for practical reasons, that policy has highlighted a new upside to the clinic as a special day for fathers and sons. When he gets feedback from the dads expressing their gratitude, George is reminded of the importance of the clinic, even though it requires considerable logistical effort for an organizer in his eighties.

"One boy came all the way from Hickory," he said. "His daddy wrote me a letter that said, 'Dear Coach, I just wanted to tell you what a wonderful time we had, and I'll have to make an admission to you. I spent more time with Johnny this particular weekend than I spent with him since he was born."

And after that, I say, 'Well Lord, you still want me to do this, don't you?'"

George, urged by his friends and family who know the inside story of the untold hours he puts into his signature event every year, does ponder how long he should keep holding the hall of fame and clinic weekend. He has often said he thinks he will hang it up when he reaches his fiftieth clinic, which would have occurred in January 2022 but will now be in 2023 since the forty-ninth event was pushed back a year due to the pandemic. With that possible deadline in mind, he brainstorms his annual hall of fame honorees with particular urgency, wanting to honor everyone he knows who is worthy but knowing that the opportunities to do so may be limited.

The impending conclusion of the annual hall of fame recognitions is one key reason why the list of George's inductees keeps getting longer and more diverse, but it isn't the only reason. The longer he presides over the Friday night ceremony, the more expansive his vision for the tradition becomes. Over thirty-five years, he has been gratified by the response of friends and strangers alike, from distinct corners of the world of sports and beyond. George's awareness of how many people deserve recognition, and their appreciation for the gesture, only broadens over time.

"I try to honor some people that have probably been forgotten about," he said. "And I try to invite people that have had wonderful careers that may have been overlooked. And every one of them seem to be shocked that I would call them, and so honored that they would be asked. Most of these people's names would pop up in my mind when I was in the shower. Just come out of nowhere, I don't know how they came into my mind. They just came to my mind and the minute they come to my mind I go call them."

George only remembers being truly nervous to make one

of those calls one time, when he reached out to former Duke basketball coach Vic Bubas. He had always had great respect for Bubas, who from 1959 to 1969 laid the groundwork for the dominance that now characterizes Blue Devil basketball. But Bubas, who died in 2018, couldn't have been more gracious. "He's the one person that I called that I was actually petrified to call," George said. "And he said, 'George? I know about your clinic, some of my boys have been honored. I'll be there!' Just like that."

In the early years, many of his honorees were top coaches and athletes from his own experiences, close friends and colleagues like Clyde King (class of 1986), Walter Rabb (class of 1987), and Hal Stewart (class of 1994). He has also always delighted in the opportunity to recognize former players who went on from Goldsboro, Richmond County or one of his college stops to even greater success. Nearly every class includes at least one member of the fraternity known as "George's boys," and in the first decade of the hall of fame alone he was able to honor Jimmy Bryan, Rooster Narron, Paul Faulk, Franklin Stubbs and Wayne Sullivan.

Every group also contains at least one name that anyone with a working knowledge of North Carolina sports history would appreciate, and one of the particular charms of George's hall of fame is the fact that members of a college basketball national championship squad are mixed in with high school golf coaches in an egalitarian blend. Those who follow ACC basketball history would have spotted such early-league standouts as David Thompson, Lou Pucillo, Steve Vacendak, Vic Molodet, Jack Murdock, Joe Quigg, Pete Brennan, and Lennie Rosenbluth at George's event. (The latter five, from N.C. State, Wake Forest and three starters from UNC's undefeated 1957 national championship team, respectively, were all honored on the same night in 2010.) From the college basketball coaching annals, men like Dave Odom (WFU), Vic Bubas (Duke), Bucky Waters (West Virginia and Duke), Terry Holland (Virginia), Les Robinson (N.C. State) and Bill Guthridge (UNC) have crossed the stage to receive one of George's plaques.

Other national or regional legends who have had their moment in the sun either at Goldsboro High School or, from 2019 on, at Wayne Community College, were Roman Gabriel and Leo Hart from the football world, Trot Nixon and Joe West from Major League Baseball and even sports journalists like A.J. Carr and Lenox Rawlings. In addition to the individual honorees, George often brings in a team that has won a state championship in recent years, or even a team observing an anniversary of an earlier accomplishment. When the 1955 Wake Forest baseball team—the only baseball national champion in the school's history—was selected for induction in 2010, thirteen former players made the trip to Goldsboro for special recognition and a team reunion.

Enabling thirteen former baseball champions in their late seventies to relive an extraordinary season was a rewarding experience for George, and year after year he has found similar sources of encouragement—moments of gratitude and connection that fortify his original vision for the annual event. Those stories, and the light in the eyes of the people who come up to be honored, make it exceedingly hard to consider ending the tradition. And he keeps finding new ways to make the evening unforgettable. In recent years the programs have taken inspirational side roads by aiming the spotlight on special-needs athletes, military heroes and even country music legends.

For the past two years, George has reached out to the N.C. Special Olympics chapter to get the name of an athlete to recognize in the hall of fame, and those individuals have provided some of the most unforgettable moments in recent memory. In 2019 a young swimmer named Bryan Henry was honored, and he was able to speak from the stage about an opportunity he would have soon to compete at the Special Olympics World Games in Dubai. As Mary Lou Ward said, "He had everybody on the edge of their seats." In 2020 the Special Olympics inductee was a 34-year-old multi-sport athlete named Ryan Hood from right there in Goldsboro, and the upcoming hall of fame class, to be recognized in January 2022, will also include a Special Olympics recipient.

As a great admirer of courageous military officers, George resolved before the 2011 ceremony that he would try to start including meritorious military award winners in his hall of fame rosters. That January he honored retired Col. Walter J. Marm, who was awarded the Medal of Honor for breaking an enemy assault at the 1965 Battle of Ia Drang in South Vietnam. Karl Eikenberry, a Goldsboro native who served as the U.S. Ambassador to Afghanistan from 2009 to 2011, was also recognized that year, and their presence at the event put George on a quest to find other military heroes whose stories deserved to be told.

Since Marm's induction a decade ago, George has included military leaders in every one of his hall of fame classes, including three more Medal of Honor recipients. When soldiers or sailors are awarded the Medal of Honor, they are given one hundred commemorative medals to give out to friends and family, and among George's treasures in his "home museum" are four such medals from the military figures who made the trip to Goldsboro for his unique ceremony.

The progressive expansion of George's hall of fame tracks with the man himself; it started mostly with baseball figures in the mid-'80s, when he himself was in the midst of a baseball-centered career, then expanded to encompass every sport in the next two decades, followed by a smattering of military and other public service and finally to include some luminaries from one of George's favorite worlds—country music. It started with one of his favorite artists, the singer known as "Whispering Bill Anderson." George had become friends with former major league baseball manager Dave Bristol, and Bristol knew Anderson and suggested that George invite him to the clinic. In 2013, Whispering Bill took his place among an assortment of accomplished sports figures, and George helped to introduce his old-style country music to a new generation.

While notable people like Anderson have officially been inducted into George's hall, others are invited for the purpose of providing entertainment to the evening's guests. Two artists who have performed there more than once are Erica Jones, who sings country music standards by the likes of Patsy Cline and Connie Smith, and Milton Bullock, a Princeville, N.C. native who spent five years singing with The Platters and now refers to himself as "The Golden Platter." "George just wants everybody to be entertained," George's childhood friend Reid Parrott said about the mixture of people he invites to Goldsboro each winter. "He wants everybody to be happy."

When George honored his first class of three baseball coaches in 1985 at Richmond Senior High in Rockingham, each of the honorees was able to give a short speech and the ceremony was still over fairly quickly. Since he has always placed a strong priority in making sure the individuals in his hall have time in the spotlight, he continued to allow new inductees to speak at the ceremony for the next eighteen years, through its transition to Goldsboro High School in 1990, until a change was necessitated in 2003 when his friend Bill Carson had his turn at the microphone.

Carson, who spent forty years as the head track coach at East Carolina and sat in the weekly Bible study with George and others at Keith LeClair's house in the final years of the young coach's life, had an extraordinary career in his sports and many moments worth honoring. He loved to talk about his athletes and his career, so when he walked to the podium to accept his plaque and was invited to say a few words he grabbed the opportunity with all the enthusiasm of a coach whose sport rarely gets a moment in the sun. "I'm going to tell you what, he talked for forty-nine minutes," George said of his friend Bill, who died in 2012. "It was Bill's chance to thank his boys. He never got much recognition, so he had a good time. That ended it. Everybody told me, they said, 'We've got to cut it short.'"

For a while after that, the inductees were still given the floor but then George made every effort to keep their remarks brief. Eventually, as each year's class swelled past twenty, George and his friends who helped him manage the clinic decided to remove the individual speeches. But one aspect of the night that George will never compromise, a detail that makes it a true hall of fame induction, is the opportunity for each individual to sit in a place of honor while his or her accomplishments are read to the audience.

"We walked in and it was packed, and I could not believe it," said Sam Story, who won two state championships in his twenty-nine-year career as the head football coach at Williams High in Burlington. "And then to sit on the stage and be honored with so many people that I had heard about, it's just something I'll never forget. It's one of the best moments of my life, to be honored by George Whitfield."

So moved was Story by the experience that he, along with untold others in George's circle, helped recommend worthy individuals for future hall of fame classes. One respected friend he nominated, longtime Cummings High School head track coach Donnie Davis, is slated to be inducted in the next class. Like Bill Carson before him, Davis has given his life to a sport that attracts very few headlines, but he has made a tremendous difference in the lives of his athletes while earning an astonishing twenty-eight state titles between the Cummings girls and boys teams. With credentials like that, George recognized that Donnie's career was the type that deserved elevating, and he gave Davis a call one day in the fall of 2020. Davis won't soon forget what it felt like to get George's surprising news. "It's a great honor any time you have someone who recognizes what you've done, your body of work," Davis said. "You really don't think of things like this while you're doing it. But when you're surprised by something like this, it's really an honor."

Like thirty other individuals including long-time UNC-Charlotte athletic director Judy Rose, Kinston High basketball coach Perry Tyndall and George's Parrott Academy headmaster Dr. Bert Bright, Davis will have to wait out the COVID-19 pandemic before walking on the stage to receive his plaque. But George wanted the full ceremony, with as many of his honorees' family members as possible to be in attendance, both because it's the only time some of them will be in a hall of fame spotlight and because George knows that the weekend that has occupied a permanent place on so many calendars can't continue forever.

"My goal is probably to get to the fiftieth," he said. "If I had to be honest, I'd say for a long time down in my heart I always said well, if I'm at forty-two, maybe I'll make it to forty-five, and forty-five maybe I'll make it to fifty. So if the good Lord wants me to do it, I always say, 'Lord, if you want me to stop, all you've got to do is throw a monkey wrench in there, and when you do I'll know it's time to hang it up.'"

Without question George has always been the engine that makes the weekend go and the inspiration behind the hall of fame selections and the clinic staff, but over the years he has developed a team to help him manage the details. It starts with a long list of friends who donate money to pay the operational expenses of the clinic. Some started sending George checks after their son attended the clinic or they were honored at the hall of fame, and many of those checks have kept coming for decades without interruption. Those financial gifts help pay for the facility, the food, transportation for visiting coaches and the most enduring symbol of George's hall of fame—the plaques.

The first friend who assists with the plaques is retired sportswriter A.J. Carr, one of George's closest friends and a hall of fame honoree himself. A.J. crafts the list of lifetime honors for each person so that they can be emblazoned on the plaques. For the three decades the ceremony has been held in Goldsboro, Scarlet Beamon from Awards Gallery has handled all of the engraving for the plaques—and anyone who has seen one of the awards up close knows that her workload is considerable. Each plaque measures sixteen by twenty inches and is completely filled with etched phrases summarizing that person's life and career.

George used to do the research on each honoree himself and decide what to list on the plaque, but after laboring over those biographies for a while he decided it would be best to ask each individual which life events they wished to highlight. It was an approach that was validated in 2009 with the induction of former Duke basketball star Steve Vacendak. George sent Vacendak his standard questionnaire asking for his accomplishments, and one of the first thing Vacendak noted was earning his Eagle Scout distinction in high school. George knew that if it had been up to him he would have focused on Vacendak's time with the Blue Devils, in the NBA, or as a college coach. But by letting Vacendak take charge of his own recognition, he emphasized something that still meant a great deal to him fifty years later. "It was the top thrill of his life over playing in the national championship for Coach Vic Bubas," George said. "And right then I said, 'No more.' I said, 'I will get in touch with them, because Steve, there's no way that I would've ever known that you were an Eagle Scout if you hadn't put it on that sheet.' And that was the most important thing."

Joining A.J. with the stack of completed questionnaires and Scarlet as she tries not to wear out her engraving machine each year are others who make the weekend go, like Donna Grady, who stepped in to handle the database and mail out hundreds of flyers for George's clinics after friends and family told him that he needed a break from addressing each envelope by hand. His son Gef and good friends Wes Waller and Kenny Coley are always his right-hand men during the hall of fame ceremony, helping organize and distribute the plaques, and a circle of close friends and family provide set-up, clean-up and other support throughout the weekend. It is George's labor of love, but those who love him most do what they can to keep it going and take some of the logistical tasks out of his hands. The support team that has formed to help enable George's favorite annual event is an apt microcosm of the love that has upheld him through his life and career.

The sustaining framework for George, as a coach, father, husband and friend, has been the relationships that each stop along the way have facilitated. He doesn't ever lose touch with anyone, but somehow keeps making room for new people who receive phone calls, chocolate-covered almonds at Christmas, and invitations to steak dinners. George is quick to point out that his family has made untold sacrifices so that he could teach baseball and life to hundreds of his "boys" from 1959 to 2015. The grace and love his inner circle has supplied to a former orphan who once flagged down a truck driver to run away from boarding school is the fuel that has allowed George to enfold so many into his chosen family over the decades.

APPENDIX 1:

People Honored at Baseball Clinics

George, far right, at his 1996 hall of fame presentation with, from left, Ed Wyatt, Steve Winchester and V.T. Craddock

1985
Bill Wilhelm*
Jack Stallings*
Chuck Hartman*

1986
Clyde King*
Ron Polk
Russ Frazier
Sam Esposito*

1987
Walter Rabb*
Earl Smith*
Stuart Maynard*
George Scherger*

1988
Augie Garrido*
June Raines
Boyd Coffie*
Jay Bergman
Robert Sapp
Dr. Al Proctor

1989
Joe Ferebee
Dr. Ron Christopher*
James Fulghum
Bob Wren*
Bobby Richardson

1990
Rick Jones
Mike Fox
Linwood Hedgepeth
Jim Ward*
Wilbur Snipes*

1991
Bill Brooks*
Mike Roberts
Ronald Vincent
Bob Bradley*
Bill Wilhelm*

1992
North Johnson
Sam Narron*
Tom Austin
Doyle Whitfield

1993
Dell Webb*
Gerald Griffin
Mark Johnson
Jimmy Bryan
Rooster Narron
Jack Stallings*
Chuck Hartman*

1994
Hal Stewart
Gary Overton
Vern Benson*
Ray Tanner
Paul Faulk

1995
Albert Long*
Brian Doyle
Hal Stewart, Sr.*
Jack McKeon

Franklin Stubbs
Jerry Narron
Wayne Sullivan
Joe West

1996
Rip Tutor*
Gilbert Ferrell
Ray Brayboy
Greg Biagini*
Jim Morris
Crash Craddock*
Ray Bunch
Ed Wyatt
Steve Winchester
Jim Morris
Keith Madison
Dr. W.C. Sanderson*

1997
Mickey McClenny*
Lee Gliarmis*
Carl Lancaster
Gerald Whisenhunt
Dr. Ricky Watkinds
Tim Stevens
Dudley Whitley*
C.W. Twiford*
Johnny Hunton
George Williams*
Jim Mallory*
Ray Pennington*
"Moe" Bauer*
Skeet Thomas
Dwight Lowery*
Claude Kennedy

1998
Ray Wilson Scarborough*
Howard McCullough
Dick Knox
Drew Coble
Carlton Frederick*
Mike Caldwell
Tracy Woodson
Wayne Lassiter
Tony Guzzo

Bob Waller
Pat Watkins
Marvin Jarman

1999
Scott Bankhead
Dave Thomas*
Ronald Scott
Don Saine
Henry Jones
Bernie Capps*
Jerry Johnson
Jimmy Williams
Dink Mills
Tom Northington
Charlie Spivey
George Greer
Roger Watson
Tony Cloninger*
Syd Thrift*
Dave McClenny*
Nelson Best*
Ron Hastings
Clyde King*

2000
A. J. Carr
Don Rood*
Charles Coburn*
Red McDaniel
George Altman
John Allen Farfour*
John Thomas*
Charlie Adams*
John Lotz*
Glenn Gregson
Louis Breeden
Henry Vansant*
Danny Talbott*
Layton Getsinger
Jerry Carter
W. D. McRoy*
Tommy Cole
Russ Frazier
Jack Stallings*

2001
Dick Baddour
Ralph Robertson
General Ron Griffith*
Missy Barrow Culbreth
Clyde Miller*
Paul B. Gay
Steve Bryant
Bobby Hodges*
Frank Weedon*
Jerry McGee*
Dave Odom
Dave Littlefield
Bryant Aldridge*
Fran Hooks
Dr. Gene Hooks
Herm Starrette
Babe Howell*
Leo Hart

2002
Dick Birmingham*
Carl Bolick*
Alton G. Brooks*
Bill Carver
Ronnie Chavis
Jack Groce
Norma Jean Harbin
Tommy John
Keith LeClair*
Harry Lee Lloyd, Jr.
Don Patrick
Rick Strunk
Henry Trevathan
Fred Williams
Walter Williams*

2003
Doug Bruton*
Bill Carson*
Calvin Daniels
Pete Dunn
Harold Ellen*
Danny Kepley
Jack Leggett
Charlie Lewis
Guy Mendenhall*

Ray Oxendine
Danny Price
Clarence Rose
Ron Sebastian
Ann Webb*
Walt Wiggins
Bob Brooks*
Norman Clark
Bill Eustler*
Dr. John Horne*
Trot Nixon
Johnny Oates*
Bobby Wilson*

2004

Willie Bradshaw*
Tim Brayboy
Boyce Dietz
Bobby Frederick
Gary Frederick
Curtis Frye
Gary Gilmore
Pat Harrell*
Dave Harris*
Gen. John M. Keane
Dr. Danny Lotz*
Dr. Jerry E. McGee
Joe Miller*
Bobby Myrick
Harold Robinson
Richard Sarmiento
Carolyn Shannonhouse
Earl Vaughan
Dr. Jim Hemby*

2005

Bruce Bolick
Harvey Brooks*
Neil Buie
Roger Dixon
Roman Gabriel
Ralph E. Holloway, Jr.
Randy Ledford*
Billy Lee
Ed Peeler
Bobby Poss
Ned Sampson*

Bob Sawyer
Pete Shankle*
Tom Smith
Kathy Stefanou

2006

Herb Appenzeller*
Dave Bristol
Alex Cosmidis*
Donnie Frederick
Larry Frederick*
R. L. Gurley*
Terry Holland
Oval Jaynes
Bill Kemp*
Fred Lanford
Dixon Sauls
Que Tucker

2007

Joe Carbone
Dr. Jimmie Grimsley*
Bob Harris
Fred Jordan
Mike Myrick
Kristi Overton Johnson
General Binford Peay, III
Lou Pucillo
Don Stallings
Jimmy Tillman
Jerry Woodside

2008

Elliott Avent
Edward "Gene" Causby*
Ed Emory*
Bobby Guthrie
Dave Jauss
Debbie Purvis Keel
Kenny K. Moore
Glenn Nixon*
Vickie Kirk Peoples
Nolan Respess
Bobby Ross
Mark Scalf
Rocket Wheeler
Dr. Alan White

2009

Tom Butters*
Clay Council
Bill Dooley*
Reese Edwards
Alley. L. Hart
Jack Holley*
B. W. Holt
Tommy Mattocks
Paul Miller
Gil Minor
Brian Moehler
Bob Murphrey
Tom Parham
Add Penfield*
Steve Vacendak
John E. Warren
Mike Winbush

2010

Billy Barnes
Daryl Barnes
Pete Brennan*
Steve Brown
Vic Bubas*
Chris Cammack*
A. J. Carr
Mark Clark
Bill Clingan
Bobby Dawson*
Bill Hensley
Marion Kirby
Lindsey Linker
Vic Molodet
Jack Murdock
Joe Quigg
Lennie Rosenbluth
Bucky Waters
Scott Wedemeyer
Goldsboro Earthquake
Teams of 1976-77

2011

Charlie Adams*
Charlie Bryant
Chris Corchiani
Carlester Crumpler

Fisher DeBerry
Karl W. Eikenberry
Ron Frederick
Bill Guthridge*
Felix Harvey*
Bill Hull*
Rock Lee*
Larry Lindsey
Jack Marin
Walter J. Marm
Don McCauley
Bill Merrifield
Jeff Mullins
Troy W. Pate, Jr.
Eddie Radford
Les Robinson
Jimmy Smith
Jan Stanley
Mike Terrell
Al Vaughan

2012

Andy Andrews
Richard Bell
Wilt Browning
Carol Carson
Wes Chesson
Bill Davis*
Woody Durham*
Maj. General Alfred K. Flowers
Ron Fly
Wells Gulledge
Mark Johnson
Bob Kennel
Ray Korn
Mac Morris
Wendell Murphy
Richard Pridgen
Bill Rowe
Don Shea*
Carl Tacy*
Dr. Tim Taft
David Thompson
David Thornton
Jerry Tolley
Bobby Vaughan

159

Lindsay Warren*
Tony Womack
Larry Worsley
Robert M. Patterson

2013

Bill Anderson
Donnie Baxter
Al Buehler
Fred Combs
Melissa Barrow Culbreth
Johnny Evans
Ching Eikenberry
Barry Hall*
Ed Hiatt*
Tommy Hunt
Jack Huss
Col. Jeannie Leavitt
Joel Long
Shelly W. Marsh
Jack McGinley
Jerry Moore
Hugh Pollock
Bobby Purcell
Gordon R. Roberts
Carolyn Rogers
Milton Senter
Moyer Smith
Nelson Smith
Anthony Teachey
Phil Weaver
Bobby Wolfe

2014

Ronnie Battle*
Sheila Boles
Ken Browning
M. L. Carr
Jeff Charles
Bill Ellis
Gary Farmer
Buck Fichter*
John Frye
Billy Godwin
Fred Goldsmith
Julie Griffin
Bob Kanaby

Jerry Kanter
Norma King*
Maj. General Steven L. Kwast
Tommy Lewis
Neill McGeachy, Jr.*
Sam Narron
John Peacock*
Mike Rabon
Joan Riggs
Ronnie Ross
Wilbur Shirley
Willie Taylor
Greg Warren
Jerry Winterton
Hilda Worthington*

2015

Eddie Biedenbach
Gil Bowman
Mickey Bridgers
Bob Catapano
Ricky Crumpler
Don Fish
Jimmy Fleming*
Millie Hall
Darrell Harrison
Rick Kobe
Clebe McClary
Wes Seegars
Monte Sherrill
Sam Story
Tom Suiter
Chad Tracy
Sue Walsh
John Williamson
Gary York

2016

Dr. Lee Adams
Wiley Barrett
Alton V. Britt, Jr.
Mike Brown
Donald Clark
Dennis Craddock*
Enid Drake
Nora Lynn Finch

Mindy Ballou Fitzpatrick
Phil Ford
Harry Frye
Cliff Godwin
Larry Honeycutt
Mike Kennedy
Chris Norman
Sherry Norris
Ray Price*
Lenox Rawlings
Si Seymour
Wade M. Smith
Dexter Williams

2017
Rob Burke*
Norm Chambers*
Chris Combs*
Charles Davis
Tommy Eason
Jabo Fulghum
Sandy Gann
Mel Gibson
Herb Goins
Helen Goldsby
Ned Gonet
Arnold Gordon-Bray
Eddie Gray
Buddy Green
Leroy Holden
Stan Johnson
Paul Kostacopulus
Bill Lam
Joey Price
Terry Rogers
Glenn Sasser
Bill Stone
Dr. David T. Taylor, Jr.

2018
Robbie Allen
Frances 'Fran' Davis Allison
Maj. General Al Aycock
Hal Bagwell
Scott Barringer
Sheilah Cotton
Kim Cousar

Bob Dailey
Reid Davis
Randy Denton
Jim Gantt
Sylvia Hatchell
David Howie
Bob Lewis
Bob McRae
Bronswell Patrick
Bob Paroli
Jim Ritcher
David W. Rothwell
Bill Rowland
Steve Spivey
Richard Sykes
Rosie Thompson
Pat Teague
Doug Watts
Brian Weingartz
Jim McCloughan

2019
Donald Andrews
Garrett Blackwelder
Jim Brett
Bill Bryan
Bill Cain
Dick Cooke
Mac Cumbo
Ivan D. Daniels
Cissy Bristol Dyer
Chip Gill
Jeff Gravely
Bob Guzzo
Joey Hackett
Loren Hibbs
Pepper Hines
Maj. General (Ret.) Dutch Holland
Dr. Charles E. Kernodle, Jr.*
Phil J. Kirk, Jr.
Charlie Long
Fred McDaniel
Angie Miller
Darrell Moody
Bill Morningstar
Joe Pate

Dale Gordon Patrick
Marc Payne
David Perry

2020
Ethan Albright
Erik Bakich
Billy Best
Hill Carrow
Kenny Dickerson
William "Bill" Fiarcloth
Barbara Foxx
David Gentry
Dino Hackett
Dr. H. Tyson Jennette
Martin Lancaster
Boyd Lee
Monte Little
Richard McGeorge
Dr. Claude Tee Moorman, III
Coach Don Osborne
Coach Lindsay Page
Corey Scott
Dr. Reginald Sherard
Coach Bill Slayton
Brandon Spoon
Coach Jimmy Teague
Coach Henry Trevathan, Jr.
Coach Curtis Walker
Brent Walters
Billy Warren
Wanda Watkins
Todd Wilkinson

2021
Jim Adkins
Gus Andrews
Philip A. Baddour, Jr.
David Ball
Karen Barefoot
Mark Barnes
Dr. Bert Bright
Everett Cameron
Chris Castor
Shelton Chesson
Tommy Cole
Donnie Davis
Eddie Gwaltney
John Haggerty
Bill Hays
Craig Hill
Rusty Lee
Jim McCloughan
Jason Mills
Jim Montague
Steve Postan
George Robinson
Chris Roehmer
Judy Rose
Ben Sutton
Dr. Earl Trevathan
Roy Turner
Perry Tyndall
Brinkley Wagstaff
Rusty Wagstaff
Nat Walker
David Weil
George Williams

APPENDIX 2:

George Whitfield's State Championship Teams

1963 Goldsboro Post 11 Lost to Greensboro Cone
4 games to 2 Won 26, Lost 10

1964 Goldsboro Post 11 Lost to Charlotte Post 9
4 games to 2 They won National Championship
Won 24, Lost 11

1968 Hamlet High School Defeated Bowman High School
2 games to 1

State AAA Champions Won 22, Lost 3

1972 Hamlet Post 49 Defeated Gastonia Post 23-198
4 games to 1 Won 35, Lost 6

1973 Richmond Senior High School
Defeated South Stokes High School
2 games to 0

State AAA Champions Won 25, Lost 2

1974 Richmond Senior High School
Defeated Durham High School
2 games to 0

State AAAA Champions   Won 25, Lost 1

1976 Richmond Senior High School
      Defeated Charlotte Garinger
      2 games to 1

State AAAA Champions
Won 27, Lost 2

1978 Hamlet Post 49   Lost to Asheboro Post 45
      4 games to 2   Won 31, Lost 11

1979 Hamlet Post 49   Defeated Rowan County Post 342
      4 games to 3   Won 36, Lost 12

1982 Hamlet Post 49   Defeated Cherryville Post 100
      4 games to 3   Won 34, Lost 17

1983 Hamlet Post 49   Defeated Charlotte Post 262
      4 games to 0   Won Southeastern Regional

World Series – Fargo, N.D.
Won 36, Lost 17

2015 Arendell Parrot Academy
      Defeated Harrell's Academy
      2 games to 0

NCISAA State AA Champions
Won 19, Lost 5

Goldsboro Post 11
State Runners-Up
Won 26, Lost 10

1963

Johnny Biddle	Danny Southerland
Jimmy Bryan	Bill Starr
Danny Dionis*	Eddie Stewart
Monty Freeken	Jimmy Stewart*
Richard Narron	Wayne Sullivan
Harry Sasser	Denny Sutton
Mike Sasser	Doyle Whitfield
Russ Sears	Eddie Wyatt

V. T. Craddock, Assistant Coach*
George F. Whitfield, Head Coach

Goldsboro Post 11
State Runners-Up
Won 24, Lost 11

1964

Bob Blanton	Mike Parrell
Jimmy Bryan	Homer Pike
Ray Bunch	Russ Sears
Mike Cole	Eddie Stewart
Frankie Hill*	Jimmy Stewart*
Timothy Howell*	Wayne Sullivan
Billy Mooring*	Eddie Wyatt
Richard Narron	

Charles Watson, Manager
Roger Watson, Manager
Hal Stewart, Assistant Coach
George F. Whitfield, Head Coach

Hamlet High School
State AAA Champions
Won 22, Lost 3

1968

John Adeimy	Lee Meacham
Mike Bolch	Jerry Mills
Buddy Coble	Mark Selph
Frank Folger	Larry Stinson
Glenn Gregson	Jerry Suggs
Bill Griggs*	Eddie Tomlinson
Terry Howe	Gratten White
Richard Knopp	Gary Wilson
Jimmy McKeithan	Steve Winchester

Cecil C. Gordon, Jr., Manager
George Huff, Manager
Johnny Kendall, Manager
Larry Weatherly, Assistant Coach
George F. Whitfield, Head Coach

Hamlet High School
State AAA Champions
Won 22, Lost 3

1968

John Adeimy	Lee Meacham
Mike Bolch	Jerry Mills
Buddy Coble	Mark Selph
Frank Folger	Larry Stinson
Glenn Gregson	Jerry Suggs
Bill Griggs*	Eddie Tomlinson
Terry Howe	Gratten White
Richard Knopp	Gary Wilson
Jimmy McKeithan	Steve Winchester

Cecil C. Gordon, Jr., Manager
George Huff, Manager
Johnny Kendall, Manager
Larry Weatherly, Assistant Coach
George F. Whitfield, Head Coach

Hamlet Post 49
NC State Champions
Won 35, Lost 6

1972

Louis Breeden	Ken Kindley
Freddy Brown	Chuck McLean
Don DeMay	Randy Monroe
Gerald Dutton	Drew Morse
Paul Faulk	Robert Robinson
Eric Freeman	David Roper
Mike Hopkins*	Charlie Wall
Ben Howe	Chuck White

Gef Whitfield, Bat Boy
Pete Howe, Athletic Officer*
Hal Stewart, Assistant Coach
George F. Whitfield, Head Coach

Richmond Senior High School
State AAA Champions
Won 25, Lost 2

1973

Matt Atkinson	Terry Massagee
Freddy Brown	Henry McDuffie
Mitchell Davis	Chuck McLean
Gerald Dutton	David Roper
Arthur Gainey*	Ricky Treadaway
Colon Gilchrist	Mike Wall
Steve Hodges	John White
Ben Howe	Randy Wilkerson
Donald Marston	Ronnie Yarborough

Jerry Lamont, Manager
William Reader, Manager
Bobby Rainey, Assistant Coach*
Hal Stewart, Assistant Coach
George F. Whitfield, Head Coach

Richmond Senior High School
State AAAA Champions
Won 25, Lost 1

1974

Greg Allen*	Jeff Norton*
Larry Brower	David Quick
Charlie Davis	Luther Reader
Herbie Dawkins	Ricky Watkins
Steve Hodges	John White
Terry Massagee	Randy Wilkerson
Henry McDuffie	Ronnie Yarborough
Chuck McLean	Chris Yow
Eddie McLean	

Steve Bateman, Manager
William Reader, Manager
Doug Smith, Manager
Reggie Wise, Manager
Bobby Rainey, Assistant Coach*
Hal Stewart, Assistant Coach
George F. Whitfield, Head Coach

Richmond Senior High School
State AAAA Champions
Won 27, Lost 2

1976

Greg Allen*	Eddie Meacham
Jeff Brown	David Quick
Mark Clark	Bill Ramsey
Gary Cox*	Kenny Roller
Charlie Davis	Jeff Thomas
Harris Davis	Archie Tyson
David Gainey	Bill Ussery
Tim Lancaster	Ricky Watkins
Donnie LeGrande	Neil Williams
Mike McDuffie*	Randy Wrenn
Eddie McLean	

Frank Edens, Manager*
Sam Niemyer, Manager
Lee Williamson, Manager
Red Allen, Assistant Coach*
Paul Faulk, Assistant Coach
George F. Whitfield, Head Coach

Hamlet Post 49
State Runners-Up
Won 31, Lost 11

1978

William Alexander	Jeff Long
Johnny Brower	Frank Manship
Rocky Carpenter	Richard Murphy
Doug Cole	Kenny Roller
Ralph David	Frank Smith*
Doug High	Franklin Stubbs
Bubba Kirkley	Darrell Wallace
Marshall Little	George Winfree

George F. Whitfield, Head Coach

Hamlet Post 49
N.C. State Champions
Won 36, Lost 12

1979

William Alexander	Marshall Little
Billy Bostick	Jeff Long
Tommy Britt*	Frank Manship
Mike Campbell	Mark Norton
Steve Chamlee	Mark Ricks
Ralph David	Frank Smith*
David Jones	Franklin Stubbs
Marshall Joyner	Dwight Thomas
Bubba Kirkley	

Carlton Mumford, Manager
Ray Short, Manager*
Pete Howe, Athletic Officer*
Hal Stewart, Assistant Coach
George F. Whitfield, Head Coach

Hamlet Post 49
N.C. State Champions
Southeastern Regional Runner-Up
Won 34, Lost 17

1982

Scott Altman	Bill Jarman
Mike Byrd	Pat Jarman
Greg Cloninger	Bud Loving
Jerome Goodwin	Mike Moore
Walter Gould	Daryl Poe
Richard Heavner	Keith Reese
Eddy Hickman	Alex Wallace
Todd Hunt	Rocky Walters
Charlie Ingram	

Sammy Ballard, Manager
Carlton Mumford, Manager
Ike Howe, Athletic Officer*
Rod Ramsey, Assistant Coach
George F. Whitfield, Head Coach

Hamlet Post 49
N.C. State Champions
Southeastern Regional Champions
World Series, Fargo, ND
Won 36, Lost 17

1983

Scott Altman	Danny Mills
Mike Byrd	Mike Moore
Greg Cloninger	Red Morrison
Charlie Ingram	Daryl Poe
Tommy King	Keith Reese
Bud Loving	Alex Wallace
Heath Altman, Bat Boy	

Ike Howe, Athletic Officer*
Marshall Little, Assistant Coach
Rod Ramsey, Assistant Coach
George F. Whitfield, Head Coach

Arendell Parrott Academy
NCISAA
State AA Champions
Won 19, Lost 5

2015

Pierce Beaman	Will Lupton
Connor Bright	Spencer Matthews
Alex Henderson	Colby McLawhorn
Zack Hill	John McLawhorn
Chase Howard	McLean Piner
Josh Jackson	Zacchaeus Rasberry
Michael Jordan	Joseph Spear
Charlie King	

Freddie Bynum, Assistant Coach
William Bynum, Assistant Coach
Jerry Drake, Assistant Coach
Tate Mooring, Assistant Coach
Jamie Stallings, Assistant Coach
George F. Whitfield, Head Coach

COVERING ALL THE BASES

APPENDIX 3:
Whitfield Career Highlights

Coached in seven decades, forty-eight years

Coached at: Goldsboro Junior High, Goldsboro High School, Goldsboro American Legion Post 11, Hamlet High School, Hamlet High School, Hamlet American Legion Post 49, Richmond Senior High School, Pitt Community College, East Carolina University, Arendell Parrott Academy

973 wins and 291 losses (High School and American Legion) 77.0%

Sixteen Conference Championships

Nine State Baseball Championships: 5 in High School – 1968, 1973, 1974, 1976, 2015

4 in American Legion – 1972, 1979, 1982, 1983

Conference Coach of the Year fourteen times

Named National High School Baseball Coach of the Year – 1969 and 1974

1966 – Head Coach for the East Team in the East/West All-Star games – East won two straight

1969 – Honored by ELKS Lodge No. 392 as North Carolina High School Coach of the Year

1974 – Honored by the Professional Baseball Representatives as North Carolina High School Coach of the Year

1980 – Elected to the North Carolina American Legion Hall of Fame

1980 – Received the Governor's Baseball Award from Governor James B. Hunt, Jr.

1980 – Received the "Order of the Long Leaf Pine" from Governor James B. Hunt, Jr.

1982 – Elected to the United States Achievement Academy Hall of Fame

1983 – Selected Head Coach of the South Team in National Sport Festival V held in Colorado Springs, CO

1986 – Selected Head Baseball Coach of Area 2 for the State Games of North Carolina held in Chapel Hill. Team won Gold Medal

1986 – Selected Athletic Director of the Year in Region IV

1987 – Honored by Scholastic Coach Magazine and Franklin Life with a Gold Coach Award as one of the Winningest Baseball Coaches in America
1988 – Received the North Carolina High School Athletic Association Distinguished Service Award

1989 – Selected North Carolina Athletic Director of the Year

1993 – Inducted into the American Baseball Coaches Association Hall of Fame in Atlanta, GA, January 9, 1993

1993 – Inducted into the Goldsboro High School Hall of Fame, January 30, 1993

1993 – Inducted into the North Carolina High School Athletic Association Hall of Fame, November 6, 1993

1999 – Inducted into the North Carolina High School Athletic Directors Hall of Fame, April 11, 1999

2000 – NCHSAA People's Choice Winner – Region IV

2002 – Received the President's Award from Pitt-Greenville Hot Stove League for many years of dedication, service, and giving of oneself to the Youth of North Carolina

2004 – Selected as one of the 90 Most Influential People in the history of high school sports in North Carolina by the NHSAA in May

2005 – Inducted into the North Carolina Sports Hall of Fame, May 19, 2005

2007 – Inducted into the Kinston/Lenoir County Sports Hall of Fame

2008 – Inducted into the Inaugural Class of the North Carolina Baseball Coaches Association Hall of Fame, January 26, 2008

2011 – Named "Tar Heel of the Week" by the News & Observer on February 6, 2011

2013 – East Carolina Alumni Association Outstanding Alumni Award, October 18, 2013

2014 – North Carolina High School Athletic Association Centennial Celebration – 100 Coaches to Remember

2014 – Inducted into the University of Mount Olive Athletics Hall of Fame on November 22, 2014

2015 – Received the Clyde King Excellence in Coaching Award from the Wilson Hot Stove League

2016 – Boy Scouts of America Distinguished Citizen Award, August 24, 2016

Over 90 players received baseball scholarships

Three Major League Players: Franklin Stubbs, Brian Moehler, Alvin Morman

2019 – Entranceway to Grangier Stadium names George Whitfield Way, September 7, 2019

COVERING ALL THE BASES

Acknowledgements

I knew George Whitfield was special the first time I met him, when we met at Starbucks in the summer of 2009 to talk about Keith LeClair. I was interviewing George for my first book, "Coaching Third: The Keith LeClair Story," and the depth of his care for LeClair and everyone in his life was quickly evident. A few months later he was inviting me to promote the book at his 2010 clinic and hall of fame ceremony, and even though I hesitated to speak at the podium after greats like Lennie Rosenbluth and Jack Murdock had accepted their plaques, I did it anyway because, as everyone knows, you don't say "no" to George.

Soon George became my first phone call for any book project with a historical sports angle. He didn't just know baseball people or people in the East; he knew *everybody* I might need to talk to in any sport, and chances were excellent he had their phone numbers written on a yellow legal pad. My husband and I started looking forward to that legendary hall of fame ceremony every January, and at some point, as I got to know more of George's friends, we started to talk about making him the subject of his own book. He was resistant to the spotlight at first, but when we convinced him that by telling his story we would highlight the stories of countless former players too, he agreed to this project.

The first list of names George supplied, when I commenced my interviews, included about 135 people from every stage of his long and varied career. When I told him that we didn't really want the research to take multiple years, he agreed to let me narrow it down a bit. One of George's fears through this process was that someone would be left out, and if you know how large his "inner circle" is you understand that leaving someone out is a guarantee unless we were going to publish several volumes. If you had stories and we didn't get to you, know that you were in George's heart, and make sure you reach out to him to share your memories directly.

One of the aspects of this project I enjoyed the most, aside from the obvious joy of listening to George Whitfield stories every day, was the range of ages represented in the ranks of "George's boys." The oldest former players, from Goldsboro in the late '50s, are nearing eighty today, while the youngest, from Parrott Academy, are twenty-one and still in college. Talk about an extensive breadth of impact.

There were certainly key players in George's story I didn't get to meet, men like Amos Sexton, Frank Mock and Bill Fay. But plenty of George's childhood friends were able to share his significant contribution to the legacy of Kinston and Red Devil athletics. My thanks to Reid Parrott, Ray Barbre, Alley Hart, Frances Mock, Wells Gulledge, Leo Hart, and Charles Lewis.

From George's Goldsboro years, I was fortunate enough to talk to Jim Fields, Bud Andrews, Dave Odom, Hal Stewart, Eddie Stewart, Johnny Peacock, Ken Johnson, Rooster Narron, Robert Taylor, Ray Bunch, and Wayne Sullivan.

I could have talked to a thousand former players and other friends from the Whitfields' decades in Richmond County, and all would have had something rich to add. The following people represented the masses and did it well: Scott Altman, David Roper, Paul Faulk, Franklin Stubbs, Gerald Dutton,

Larry Stinson, Larry Riggan, Louis Breeden, Brian Moehler, Alvin Morman, Ralph Robertson, Rod Ramsey, Richard Knopp, Ruben Wall, Steve Winchester, Franklin Stubbs, and Alex Wallace. From that one year at Mississippi State, Ron Polk and Mark Johnson were more than happy to talk about their former Bulldogs colleague and friend.

After he left Hamlet, George undertook three consecutive coaching and athletic leadership challenges at the college level, and the following friends from those days provide valuable insight and anecdotes: Carl Lancaster from Mount Olive, Monte Little, Cory Scott and Jamie Stallings from Pitt Community College, and Erik Bakich, Nick Schnabel, Cliff Godwin, Link Jarrett, Billy Godwin, Sam Narron, and John Williamson from East Carolina. From the final stop, George's Parrott Academy championship cherry on top of a decadent and rewarding coaching career, I relied on Bert Bright, Connor Bright, Jamie Stallings, Tate Mooring and Zaccheus Rasberry. Other friends, including A.J. Carr, Gil Minor, Don Fish, Sam Story, Donnie Davis, Steve Spivey, and Bob Kennel, shared memories from travels with George and gave insight into his annual hall of fame festivities.

At the center of this book, of course, are George and his patient and supportive family. Mary Lou facilitated numerous editing sessions with George (even agreeing to FaceTime me a few times in the midst of the pandemic), talked through endless details and even loaned me her beautiful Emerald Isle condo for a winter writing retreat. And Tyler and Gef assisted with pictures and stories, making every effort to help create a fitting tribute to their extraordinary dad.

None of this would have come to pass without two of George's oldest friends, Claude Kennedy and Reid Parrott, who finally decided that we had talked about a book long enough and it was time to make it real. They listened to me when I explained what it would take to make this book as winning as George's teams were for so many decades, and I'm so glad I was invited to join the fun. And finally, I owe my heart and my deepest thanks to my own biggest cheerleaders, my husband Sid and my children Preston, Holly, Ben and Jake. Preston and Holly aren't just wonderful daughters; they are also top-notch publishing assistants on transcription and other tasks that were crucial to turning the book out in a short timeframe. Like George, I am blessed indeed.

George's parents, Dr. George and Marie Whitfield

George and his sister Catherine with their "mama" Ada Haines after the death of their mother Marie.

George with his father in 1948, when George was twelve. His father died later that year.

George's adoptive father Amos Sexton with all of the hardware he won as the basketball coach at Grainger High School.

Amos and Lee Sexton

Frank L. Mock Jr., George's beloved American Legion coach and football and baseball coach at Grainger High.

W.L. "Bill" Fay, the city recreation director in Kinston who befriended George and gave him a job after his father died.

George with his teammate and fellow guard Darwin Williams in 1953 at Grainger High School.

George as a freshman cadet at The Citadel.

George on his first day of coaching at Goldsboro Junior High in 1959.

Gef Whitfield with Willie Mays in 1969 on one of his visits to Yankee Stadium with his dad.

George and future college basketball coaching legend Dave Odom coaching the Goldsboro Earthquake baseball team in 1966.

George with his children Tyler and Gef in 1972 after his first American Legion state title with Hamlet Post 49.

George with Paul Faulk and Hal Stewart, with whom he shared many victories in Richmond County.

George at his induction into the NCHSAA Hall of Fame in 1993.

According to George, "No coach could have a dearer friend than Clyde King."

Alvin Morman, who played for George's Hamlet American Legion team and went on to play in the major leagues.

George with Franklin Stubbs, who played for him in Hamlet and went on to win the World Series with the Dodgers in 1988.

185

Former Richmond County standout and MLB pitcher Brian Moehler with George and Ken Johnson.

Former ECU players Clayton McCullough, John Williamson, and Bryant Ward with George when the Pirates played Cal State-Fullerton.

George with Baltimore Orioles manager Buck Showalter at spring training

Gil Minor, George, General Binford Perry III and Clyde King on a trip to VMI.

Mark Johnson, Keith Madison, George and Jerry Kindall at the College World Series in Omaha.

Ronnie Sexton, George and Tate Mooring at the College World Series in Omaha.

Bill Paulette, George, Gil Minor and Clyde King on a trip to Yankee Stadium.

Lifetime friends Claude Kennedy, Ray Barbre, Reid Parrott, George and Bert Saville.

George, Felix Harvey, Mike Rouse and Clyde King at Felix Harvey's 90th birthday celebration.

George with Ray Bunch, who went from second base on George's Goldsboro team to a successful career in the music world.

George with former UNC star and assistant coach Phil Ford.

A reunion of the ECU Pirates baseball team from the late '90s.

At a banquet for N.C. Fellowship of Christian Athletes: Back row: George, Albert Long, Johnny Evans, Danny Lotz and David Wall. Front row: A.J. Carr, Clyde King and Fisher DeBerry.

George with legendary UNC basketball coach Dean Smith.

George with Eugene "Red" McDaniel – a great Red Devil and a hero of the Vietnam War.

Clyde King, Bob Griese, Don Shula, Paul Dietzel, Jerry Richardson and Mack Brown at a lunch at the Grandfather Mountain Club, an event that George attended with Clyde.

Boyhood pals Alley Hart, Ray Barbre, Gary Scarboro, George, Charlie Lewis and Bryant Aldridge.

George with Wells Gulledge, a lifelong friend who won three state basketball titles at Kinston High.

Grainger Red Devil friends Tommy Cole, Leo Hart, Alley Hart, George, Jean Aldridge, Reid Parrott and Ray Barbre.

George with his high school hero Bryant Aldridge and Bryant's wife Jean.

Gene Watson, George and Rhonda Vincent at a concert at Lenoir Community College.

Clyde and Norma King

George with his grandsons Lucas and Nicholas.

Gef, Nicholas, Mary Lou, George, Lucas, Tyler and Jon – George's biggest fans.

George with Dolly Parton backstage at Dolly's concert in Charlotte.

George with his adopted family, the Sextons -- Carol Sexton, Ed Sexton, Patti Sexton, Don Sexton and Lucy Sexton, the wife of George's late brother Ronnie Sexton.

George's children Gef and Tyler.

Mary Lou was, in George's words, "the wind beneath my wings" in Goldsboro and Richmond County.

George's sister Kathy's four children: left to right: Jim MacRae, Kappa Parnell, Marie Sutherland, Sam MacRae

At George's last game as a head coach, when Parrott defeated Harrell's Academy for the state championship, with Mary Lou, Tyler, Coach Nicholas and Lucas.

George with his sister Kathy at the Grand Ole Opry.

GATHER 'ROUND -- Pirate second baseman Bill Mazeroski and cather Jim Pagliaroni held court on the first base line for the Richmond County delegation to Forbes Field this week. Coach Whitfield and the boys were given the first class treatment all the way. (Staff Photos by Unger)

LOOKING FOR VICTORY -- Scorebook in hand, Coach George Whitfield watches the action intently as his American Legion juniors play host to Wilmington. If the Richmond County aggregation wins this evening at Hamlet Memorial Park, it's all over for the team from the Carolina coast. Richmond County has already won two series, first from Fuquay, then from Sanford.

Made in the USA
Middletown, DE
06 June 2021